Anonymous

Scottish Gaelic as a Specific Subject

Stage I

Anonymous

Scottish Gaelic as a Specific Subject
Stage I

ISBN/EAN: 9783337233655

Printed in Europe, USA, Canada, Australia, Japan

Cover: Foto ©ninafisch / pixelio.de

More available books at **www.hansebooks.com**

SCOTTISH GAELIC

AS A SPECIFIC SUBJECT.

STAGE I.

Compiled by a Committee of The Highland Association.

"*Dùisg suas, a Ghàidhlig, 's tog do ghuth.*"
N. Mac Lèoid.

PUBLISHED FOR
THE HIGHLAND ASSOCIATION
By ARCHIBALD SINCLAIR, 10 Bothwell St., Glasgow.
NORMAN MACLEOD, Edinburgh.
HUGH MACDONALD, Oban.   THOMAS BOYD, Oban.

1893.

[*Copyright.*]

PREFACE.

This Grammar is designed principally for the teaching of the Scottish Gaelic Language as a specific subject under the Education Code for Scotland; but it is meant also for other uses.

Although there are at present several Gaelic Grammars in print, it is complained that none of them is suitable for the teaching of classes. The Highland Association has therefore undertaken to prepare and publish a new one, of which this is the first part.

In the manner of treatment, the Compilers have gone off the beaten track, judging it best to exhibit the structure of the language in a way suited to itself, without having undue regard to conventional methods. The fact that teachers are not all perfectly conversant with the grammar of the language, has been kept in view. Much of the matter given is meant for their instruction and guidance, and need not necessarily be taught to very young pupils in the order in which it is set down. A good deal must be left in this way to the discretion of teachers.

Exercises in translating Gaelic into English, and *vice versa*, are given at intervals. It was considered advisable, owing to the difficulties of inflection and idiom, to introduce exercises in the translation of English into Gaelic only after inflection is entered upon, and then but sparingly.

No exercises are given in Sections I., II., and III.; but teachers, if so disposed, can use those given in the other Sections for exercising pupils in Spelling and Pronunciation.

The aim of Stage I. is to introduce to pupils the peculiar structure and tendencies of the language, leaving irregularities and other difficulties to be dealt with in Stage II., which, it is intended, shall be mainly an extension of the items taken up in Stage I.

The Vocabulary at the end of the book has been arranged to suit the exercises.

May, 1893.

GAELIC GRAMMAR.

STAGE I.

INTRODUCTION.

1. Grammar professes to classify the facts of a language, and to deduce rules for Speaking and Writing it according to current usage.

2. Language is the expression of Thought by means of Words.

3. Thoughts are made up of Ideas which can be arranged and connected in various ways for communication to other minds.

4. The Representatives of the Ideas are the Words. The Words and the Ideas are inseparable, and, apart from the mere sounds of the words in speaking and their forms in writing, whatever is true of the Word is true of the Idea. As Words change or grow, so do the Ideas, even though the changes be due to the mechanical actions of the organs of speech alone.

5. Some Ideas or Words are associated with actual things which can be seen or felt; some with the manifestations of things; and some are so vague in their nature as to have no value out of connection with other ideas. Whatever these latter may have implied in time past, they are now used, along with others, in

a conventional manner. But their presence cannot be dispensed with as elements in the construction of thought.

6. It is with the Written and Spoken words, their component elements, their construction, their changes, uses and arrangement in the expression of thought, that grammar deals; and they will be treated of in Sections, as follows:—

I. WORDS in Isolation, in regard to their Mechanical Structure and Representation.
II. WORDS in Composition, in regard to their Mechanical Changes and Representation.
III. WORDS, in regard to their Formation and Development.
IV. WORDS, in regard to the Functions they fulfil in the Expression of Thought.
V. WORDS, in regard to the Changes they undergo in fulfilling their Functions in the Expression of Thought.

7. Languages are all in a state of transition. At some stages of their development, the transition is more marked than at others. This is specially true of the Scottish Gaelic. In its case, the Vernacular has for, at most, the last two centuries, been pushing itself forward into the position formerly held by what can only, as far as the Scottish Highlands is concerned, have been a Literary Dialect. That fact accounts for a certain want of uniformity in its diction and orthography. While the language is so conditioned, grammatical rules are difficult to formulate, and, after having been formulated, cannot be expected to command strict adherence from those to whom the language is the mother tongue. However desirable uniformity may be thought to be, no new Grammar can hope to do more than assist in its attainment.

SECTION I.

WORDS IN ISOLATION.

8. Letters.—Letters are the Written Figures which represent the Spoken Sounds. In the written language, unspoken letters are numerous. Many of them were once spoken. But those now unspoken are not all useless. In the words, *bad, suas, iasg,* the whole of the letters are sounded, and none of them can be left out. In the words, *sùil, fear, ceud, diog,* the *i, a, u,* and *o,* though silent, cannot be left out, because they are needed to indicate the pronunciation of the letters which follow them. The letters *l, r, d,* and *g* have more than one sound each, and, without the silent letters preceding them, we would not know which of their sounds to give them. Silent letters were not all put into the spelling of words for the purpose of indicating the pronunciation of the letters adjoining them, but came into their places as the language changed. In the word *sàmhchair*—sounded *sàch-ir*—the *m* tells us that an *m* was originally sounded as part of the word. The *h* indicates that *m* has decayed. It is not sufficient, however, to indicate its complete silence, for *mh* in some other words, is sounded like *v* or *w,* as in *damh, amharus* —pronounced *dav, avarus* or *awarus. Mh* has therefore two values, and nothing to guide us as to which to use.

This is a defect, but it is not a serious one, for it can be overcome by the study of the relations existing between spoken and written words. Very few languages, if any at all, can boast of a perfect system of spelling, and the Gaelic language is like others in this respect. Its system is, however, much better than it gets credit for— prevailing opinions being mostly formed from insufficient knowledge.

9. **Vowels and Consonants.**—Words are made up of Sounds and Modifications of Sounds. These are called Vowels and Consonants respectively. The Vowels make a Full Sound, which may be prolonged without motion on the part of any of the organs of speech, except those in the throat actually engaged in the production of the sound. The Consonants are for the most part Modifications of Sounds, caused by the movements of the vocal organs, principally the tongue and the lips.

10. **Vowel Letters.**—The Vowel Sounds are Ten in number, and are represented by the Five letters,

a, o, u ; e, i.

11. **Consonant Letters.**—The Consonant Sounds are represented by the Letters,

c, g ; t, d, s ; l, n, r ; p, b, f, m ; h.

12. *H*, when written apart from any other letter, thus, *h-uile*, is the sign for a Strong Breathing Impulse. When it is attached to another letter its purpose is entirely different.

13. When the consonant letters are written with *h* after them they represent new sounds having definite relations to the sounds of the letters to which the *h* is attached. Those which take *h* after them are,

c, g ; t, d, s ; p, b, f, m.

14. *L, n,* and *r* have also correspondingly different sounds, which might with advantage be represented by *lh, nh,* and *rh*; but the custom of the written language is to leave it to the sense of the passages wherein they occur, to determine when they shall have their second sounds and when not. After, but not before, vowels they are sometimes written double, thus, *ll, nn, rr,* and they differ from *l, n, r,* as in *dall, ann, bàrr.*

15. It is best to regard the consonant letters, whether they be single, double, or joined to *h,* as Simple Consonants and not as Compounds, for the sounds they represent are not compound.

16. **Long and Short Vowels.**—Vowels are sounded Long and Short. The Long Vowels have a mark placed over them to distinguish them from the Short Vowels, thus,

à, ò, ó, ù ; è, é, ì.

17. The Vowel Letters *o* and *e* have each two sounds, and, when long, the distinction is indicated by the direction of the marks placed over them, as,

bròn, *grief.*   mór, *great.*
dèan, *do.*   féin, *self.*

18. These Duration Marks over *o* and *e* are not used regularly, because the pronunciation of the words in which long *o* and *e* occur, is not itself uniform over the country. The words *a* (out of) and *am* (time) are often represented *à* and *àm,* to distinguish them from other words similarly spelt, although in these words the vowel is short.

19. There is, besides the Vowel Sounds already referred to, another long one represented by the two letters *ao.*

20. **The Complete Alphabet.**—The Complete Alphabet includes all the devices used for the representation of Vowels and Consonants, and is as follows :—

VOWEL LETTERS.

SHORT, a, o, u ; e, i.   LONG, à, ao, ò, ó, ù ; è, é, ì.

CONSONANT LETTERS.

c, g ; t, d, s ; p, b, f, m ; l, n, r ; h-.
ch, gh ; th, dh, sh ; ph, bh, fh, mh ; ll, nn, rr.

H without an accompanying consonant, is never used without a hyphen following it.

21. **Pronunciation.**—The pronunciation of the Vowels may be conveyed by means of a Phonetic Alphabet, in which the values of the symbols are illustrated by certain typical words upon the pronunciation of which most people are agreed. The symbol used to represent the sound of the letter is called a Phonotype.

22. The pronunciation of the Consonants may be learned only by ear. It may be stated, however, that the pronunciation of *ph* = *f*, *dh* = *gh*, and *mh* = *bh*. *Th* and *sh* at the beginning of a word = *h*. *Fh* is silent, except in the words *fhéin, fhuair,* and *fhathast,* in which it is sounded *h*.

23. A comparison with Irish Gaelic, Welsh and English, shows that in them, the Consonants, *c, g, t, d, p,* and *b,* are enunciated with less force than the corresponding Consonants in Scottish Gaelic. English *t* in "feature," *d* in "tedious," *k* in "keen," and *c* in "cave," *g* in "give," *y* in "you," *l* in "filial," *n* in "pinion," and *sh* in "shut," are what are called in the sequel, High (or Small) Consonants, and correspond, except in regard to force in the case of some of them, to Gaelic *t* in *iteag, d* in *séididh, c* in *ceum, g* in *geur, gh* in *gheur, ll* in *maille, nn* in *bainne,* and *s* in *seas.*

24. TABLE OF VOWEL SOUNDS.

Phonotype.	Long. Gaelic Words.	English Words.	Phonotype.	Short. Gaelic Words.	English Words.
OO	ròs	dawn	O	dos	dot
AA	càs	far	A	cas	staff
*	*	*	a	agam	but
QQ	Mòrag	ore	Q	tog	coat
VV	taobh	*	V	lagh	*
UU	cùl	loose	U	rug	hook
EE	sèimh	*	E	lean	let
*	*	*	i	againn	fit
ƎƎ	fèin	rein	Ǝ	fead	face
II	cir	seethe	I	sir	leap

Asterisks occurring under "English Words," signify that there are no equivalents in English. (a) and (i) occur only in unaccented syllables, and are always short.

25. Classification of Vowel Sounds.—The Vowel Sounds are classified as Low and High according to the position of the tongue during their utterance.

26. Low and High were formerly called Broad and Small, terms having no connection with the actual facts. But to prevent misapprehension, "Broad" and "Small" will be used in brackets after "Low" and "High" on every occasion on which the terms may be required in this book.

27. **The Low Vowels.**—The Low Vowels are O, A, a, Q, V, U, and their corresponding long sounds. The Low Vowel Letters are a, o, u ; à, ò, ó, ù.

28. **The High Vowels.**—The High Vowels are E, i, Ǝ, I, and their corresponding long sounds. The High Vowel Letters are e, i ; è, é, ì.

29. O, Q, and U and their long correspondents are classed also as Labial Vowels, because the lips are concerned in giving them their character.

30. Vowels preceding or following *n* or *m*, have, as a rule, a Nasal Tone. This is the more noticeable when *n* and *m* are silent, which sometimes happens when they follow a vowel, as, *mànran, còmhradh.*

31. **Classification of Consonant Sounds.**—The Consonant Sounds are divided into two great classes called Low and High, named, like the Vowels, after the position of the tongue during their utterance. The corresponding terms "Broad" and "Small" were also formerly applied to the Consonants.

32. In the written language, High (Small) Consonants are followed, preceded or flanked by High (Small) Vowels; and Low (Broad) Consonants by Low (Broad) Vowels. The difference of pronunciation must be learned by ear. This will be materially assisted by the following classification and examples. The purpose of the Phonotypes is for future reference. The Consonant Sounds are classed and named after the organs which are instrumental in giving them their distinguishing character.

33. COMPLETE CONTACT signifies that, in the utterance of a number of the consonants, the tongue is at some time keeping back all breath by its being applied closely to some part of the inner surface of the mouth.

34. PARTIAL CONTACT means that the tongue is so applied that at no time is breath completely stopped

35. WEAK means that breath is impelled with a force weaker than that called STRONG in the next paragraph.

36. STRONG means that breath is impelled with stronger force than that last referred to.

37. LINGUAL is applied to consonants pronounced by the agency of the tongue. BACK is added when the back part of the tongue is applied at the back of the mouth. FRONT is added when the front part of the tongue is applied at the front of the mouth.

38. NASAL is used when the breath is allowed to pass out by the channel of the nose, while it is shut off in the other direction.

39. SIDE is used when the breath is allowed to escape at the sides of the tongue.

40. TRILL refers to a certain shake given to the point of the tongue.

41. FLAT is used when the point of the tongue is applied broadly.

42. SHARP is used when the point of the tongue is applied pointedly.

43. LEATHANN RI LEATHANN AGUS CAOL RI CAOL.—This is the Gaelic rule that a Consonant Letter having a Low (Broad) Vowel Letter before it, must have a Low (Broad) Vowel Letter after it; and a Consonant Letter having a High (Small) Vowel Letter before it, must have a High (Small) Vowel Letter after it. In many cases this is not at all necessary; but the rule as a general rule, is much more easily kept in its entirety than one with a large number of exceptions.

44. There are a few breaches of the rule in the language, of which the following are those which most commonly come under observation:—

   Is in which *s* is sounded Low (Broad).
   So ,, *s* ,, High (Small).
   Sud ,, *s* ,, High (Small).
   Ged ,, *d* ,, Low (Broad).
   Tigh ,, *t* ,, Low (Broad).

45. There are others which will be referred to at a more advanced stage. *Tigh, so,* and *sud* are not infrequently spelt *taigh, sco, siod.*

46. The following Additional Phonotypes are necessary to completely represent the pronunciation of the language, namely:—

 · (inverted period) for the Strong Impulse = h·.
 ' (inverted comma) for the Weak Impulse, like that with which all vowels begin.
 w for the sound of *w* in "war" and "now," before or after Low (Broad) Vowels.
 W may be used before High (Small) Vowels.

47. TABLE OF CONSONANTS—LOW.

CLASSES.	COMPLETE CONTACT.						PARTIAL CONTACT.					
	WEAK.			STRONG.			WEAK.			STRONG.		
	Phono-types.	Names.	EXAMPLES.	Phono-types.	Names.	EXAMPLES.	Phono-types.	Names.	EXAMPLES.	Phono-types.	Names.	EXAMPLES.
Back Linguals	G	ga	gabh, rag, sagart	C	ca	cas, sac, tacau	ɔ	gha	ghò, lagh, aghaidh	ᴄ	cha	chas, ach, lochan
Front "	D	da	do, rud, fada	T	ta	tom, lot, botul	s	sa	sàr, cas, dìomhsa	s'	s'a	sac, cas, guth-san
Simple Labials	B	ba	bog, gob, stàbull	P	pa	pòs, sop, tapaidh	v	bha	bha, gabh, cabhag	F	pha	phòs, fan
Nasal Labial	M	ma	mór, tom, caman									
Back Nasal	NG	ang	long, teanga									
	FLAT.						SHARP.					
Side Lingual	LL	lla	làmh, toll, cala	LL'	hlla	thlachd, shloe	L	la	mo làmh			
Trill Lingual	RR	rra	ràmh, tur, corrag	RR'	hrra	shruth, thràth	R	ra	mo rùn			
Nasal Lingual	NN	nna	nàire, ann, annam				N	na	mo nàire, fan	N'	hna	shnàth, thnù

NOTE.—The Nasal Labial and Back Nasal are "complete contact" only so far as the lips and the tongue are concerned; the nasal passage is open. In respect to the tongue, the Nasal Lingual is "complete contact"; but it and the preceding two classes are not classified in reference to contact.

48. TABLE OF CONSONANTS—HIGIL.

CLASSES.	COMPLETE CONTACT.					PARTIAL CONTACT.				
	WEAK.			STRONG.		WEAK.			STRONG.	
	Phono-types.	Names.	EXAMPLES.	Phono-types.	Names.	EXAMPLES.	Phono-types.	Names.	EXAMPLES.	Phono-types.	Names.	EXAMPLES.

CLASSES.	Phono-types.	Names.	EXAMPLES.	Phono-types.	Names.	EXAMPLES.	Phono-types.	Names.	EXAMPLES.	Phono-types.	Names.	EXAMPLES.
Back Linguals	G	gi	geum, thig, aige	C	ci	ceum, taic, reicidh	G	ghi	gheur, àigh, òighe	C·	chi	chè, teich, ciche
Front ,,	D	di	dèan, goid, idir	T	ti	tinn, duit, tuitidh	S	si	sìor, spèis, cùiseil	·S·	si	siu, nis, coise
Simple Labials	B	bi	bith, guib, caibe	P	pi	pige, cuip, suipeir	V	bhi	bhi, sibh, aibhis	F	phi	phill, fir, ifrinn
Nasal Labials	M	mi	mìr, lìm, imeachd									
Back Nasal	NG	ing	luing, aingeal									

FLAT.   SHARP.

CLASSES.	Phono-types.	Names.	EXAMPLES.				Phono-types.	Names.	EXAMPLES.	Phono-types.	Names.	EXAMPLES.
Side Lingual	LL	lli	lìon, pill, tillidh				L	li	lìon mi e, sìl, dìle	·L·	bli	shliochd
Trill Lingual	RR	rri	rìgh, oirre				R	ri	mo rìgh, fir, fìrinn	·R·	hri	shrian
Nasal Lingual	NN	nni	nìgh, tinn, iñneal				N	ni	mo neart, sìn, fìne	·N·	hni	shnìomh

NOTE.—The Nasal Labial and Back Nasal are "complete contact" only so far as the lips and the tongue are concerned; the nasal passage is open. In respect to the tongue, the Nasal Lingual is "complete contact"; but it and the preceding two classes are not classified in reference to contact. The above phonotypes are capitals to distinguish them from the small capitals of the former table.

49. Silent Vowel Letters.—When two Vowel Letters come together, and only one of them is sounded, the purpose of that which is silent is to indicate the class to which the consonant next it belongs.

50. Low (Broad) Consonants have their class indicated by *a* when the vowel is *e* and short, as, *beag, fead, leat, bean, leac*. When the Vowel *e* is long, the Silent Indicating Vowel is *u*, as, *meud, beum, feur, leus*, with exceptions such as *dèan, nèamh*. It is unusual, because unnecessary, to use the Duration Mark over *e* followed by *u*. When the vowel is *i*, long or short, the Silent Indicating Vowel is *o*, as, *ploh, fior, dìol, diog, bior*.

51. High (Small) Consonants have their class indicated by silent *i* before them as, *ait, dail, saoil, aois, sùil, muir, cuid, toil, sèul, còir, féill, seinn, ceil, sèimh*, etc.

52. **Syllables.**—Words consist of one or more distinct sounds or Syllables. In writing, Syllables are separated from one another by consonant letters; and every syllable must contain a vowel. The consonant letters may or may not be sounded; but there is always a consonant letter or letters between Written Syllables. When two syllables come together without a Spoken Consonant, but in a word which has a Silent Written Consonant, the second syllable must begin with a Weak or a Strong Impulse. This is referred to in books by the name "Hiatus," and is exemplified in the words *athair, màthair*, = A'iR or A·iR, MAA'iR.

53. Words of one syllable are called Monosyllables; of two, Dissyllables; of three, Trisyllables; and of four or more, Polysyllables. Polysyllables are few, because there is a strong tendency in the language to reduce the number of syllables in all words, but particularly in Polysyllabic Words.

54. Accent.—Syllables are classed as Accented and Unaccented. The Accented Syllables are those which are spoken with a certain stress on the voice, which is absent from the Unaccented Syllables. In words of more than one syllable, the accent is on the First Syllable. Certain small words of a connecting or indicating nature, as, *an* (the), *air* (on), are never accented. Some words of frequent occurrence are accented or unaccented according to the circumstances in which they occur; and sometimes words having Long vowels when Accented, have Short ones when Unaccented, e.g.—

Tha e beag.
Is he little. } He is little—*e* unaccented and short.

Cha 'n é.
Not he. } He is not—*é* accented and long.

Cha bhi e.
Not be he. } He will not be—*Bhi* accented and long.

Na bi feargach.
Not be angry. } Be not angry—*Bi* unaccented and short.

55. Diphthongs.—Two Vowel Sounds coming together without an Intervening Consonant or Hiatus, spoken with but one impulse, and seeming to glide into one another, or, in other words, forming one syllable, are called Diphthongs. They may be classified as follows:—

56. I.—Diphthongs of which i is the second element.

LONG.

A and i.	O and i.	V and i.	U and i.
dailbh	doimhne	craibh	duibh
aimhse	doibh	doill	tuill
laimh	cloimh	oighre	duibhre

SHORT.

daimh	troimh	cailbe	cuip
cailbeal	coimeas	eibre	suipeir

B

57. As a general rule, with some exceptions, *i* before labial consonants, *ll, nn,* and *dh* and *gh* before another consonant, is sounded as the second element of a diphthong. There are no duration marks for these diphthongs.

58. II.—Diphthongs with a Low (Broad) Vowel as the second element.

E and O.	I and a.	I and U.	U and a.
beò	fiar	fiù	buan
leòn	cian	cliù	fuar

59. The Diphthongs of this class are almost always Long. EO and IU are Short in *beothail* and *piuthar;* but short diphthongs of this class may be said to be exceptional. In the case of EO and IU, the pronunciation of the first element is slight, and many quite neglect it. In the case of Ia and Ua, the quantity is generally given to the first element.

60. **Triphthongs.**—Three Vowels coming together and sounded with the glide, are called a Triphthong. Triphthongs are few. They are almost confined to Uai before labial consonants, as, *uaibh, uaimh*. As a rule, the Third Vowel of a written group is to indicate the class to which the consonant following it belongs, as, *uair, buail, uaill, uaigh, beòir, feòil, eòin, ciùil, ciùin, stiùir, fiaire.*

61. The custom of naming two and three vowel letters Diphthongs and Triphthongs, whether they be all sounded or not, should be discontinued; and the ability to distinguish when a vowel is sounded and when its purpose is to indicate the pronunciation of the consonant, should be carefully cultivated.

62. **Silent Consonants.**—When two Vowels belonging to separate syllables come together, i.e., when a Hiatus occurs between them, they are always found in the

WORDS IN ISOLATION.

written language with Consonant Letters between them. In most cases, these consonant letters represent consonants formerly spoken. The consonant letters most frequently silent between vowels belonging to different syllables, are :—

63. *th*, as, *athair* = A'iR ; *cathag* = CA'AG ; *fuathas* = FUA'AS. But many pronounce *th* after short accented vowels, as *h*; *athair* = A·iR.

64. *dh*, as, *cridheil* = CRI'EL ; *bodhar* = BO'AR ; *stuadhan* = STUA'AN. But a better pronunciation of *dh* after long vowels is ꬴ and Ꭷ, as, *stuadhan* = STUAꬴAN ; *bòidheach* = BOOꭷAꬴ.

65. *gh, mh, bh* are sometimes silent between vowels; but it is not the best practice to follow. That is best which gives ꬴ and Ꭷ to *gh*, and V or W to *mh* and *bh*; as, *laghan* = LLVꬴAN ; *toigheach* = TVꬴAꬴ ; *labhairt* = LLAViRT ; *amharus* = AVARAS or AWARAS.

66. *th, dh, gh, mh, bh*, and *n*, after a vowel and before another consonant, are silent, as, *cathrach* = CARAꬴ ; *buidhre* = BUiiRa; *oighre* = viiRa ; *còmhla* = COOLLA ; *mànran* = MAARAN. *Samhradh, geamhradh, cabhraich*, and others of the same class, in which *mh* and *bh* follow *a*, have

67. *mh* or *bh* sounded V and W, as SAVRA or SAWRA ; GEVRA or GEWRA ; CAVRIꬴ or CAWRIꬴ.

68. *th* final is always silent, as, *cath* = CA ; *sìth* = SII.

69. *dh* final is silent before words beginning with a consonant; but is best sounded ꬴ and Ꭷ before words beginning with a vowel, as *bualadh chluch* = BUaLLa ꬴLAꬴ ; *bualadh innein* = BUaLLAꬴ iNNEN.

70. *fh* is always silent except in the words *fhéin, fhuair, fhathast*, when it is sounded like *h*, as ᴇᴇN, 'UaiR, 'A'AST.

71. Silent and Decayed Consonants are apt, from want of knowledge on the part of writers of Gaelic, to be represented at variance with the Radical Consonants from which they came. A few cases in point are—

Troigh, a foot, which some write *troidh*.
Tràigh, a shore, occasionally spelt *tràidh*.
Riamh, ever, which a number spell *riabh*.

72. **Compound Consonants.**—The Consonants represented by *l, n, r, m* and *s*, combine with others to form Compound Consonants. They are of several classes.

1. Those which precede vowels.

cr, chr; gr, ghr; tr, thr; dr, dhr; shr; pr, phr; br, bhr.
cl, chl; gl, ghl; tl, thl; dl, dhl; shl; pl, phl; bl, bhl.
cn, chn; gn, ghn; tn, thn; shn; mn, mhn.
sgr; str; spr; sgl, spl.

2. Those which follow vowels.

rc, rch; rg, rgh; rt; rd, rs; rp; rb, rbh; rn, rl, rm.
lc, lch; lg, lgh; lt; ld, ls; lp, lb, lbh; ln, lm.
nc, ng; nt, nd, ns; nm; mp, mb.
chd.

3. Those which precede or follow vowels.

sg; st; sd; sp; sb; sr; sl, sn, sm.

73. Some of the second series are pronounced with a very slight vowel sound between the components, as *deary*, DERAG; *dealy*, DELAG; *seily*, SAILG; *colbh*, COLLAV.

74. *Rd* and *rt* after Vowels are very frequently sounded *rsd, rst*, as, *bàrd*, BAARSD; *feart*, FERST; *cairt*, CARST. In general, however, only *rt* is so sounded.

75. *Thr, thl, thn; shr, shl, shn*, are pronounced *hr, hl, hn; hr, hl, hn*, respectively. *Fhr* and *fhl* have *fh* unsounded.

76. *N* after *c, ch; g, gh; t, th; m* and *mh*, is commonly pronounced like *r*, as, *cnap*, CRAP; *gnàth*, GRAA; *mnathan*, MRA'AN, etc. But this pronunciation is not to be commended: *n* should get its proper sound.

77. *Chd* is always pronounced as if spelt *chc* = ɔc.

78. **Vowels in Unaccented Syllables.**—All that has been previously stated about the vowels, applies only to those which occur in Accented Syllables. Vowels in Unaccented Syllables must have separate treatment. In the Unaccented Syllables, the vowel letters have sounds of which the spelling gives no indication. They

are always short and sometimes obscure, and there are no diphthongs or triphthongs. The Vowel Sounds V, O, Q, U and Ʊ are rarely found in Unaccented Syllables.

79. A is found in a few short unaccented words which will be referred to as they occur in the sequel, and in the syllables *an*, *ag*, and *eag*, when they mean Diminutiveness, as, *caman* = CAMAN ; *sgalag* = SGALLAG ; *caileag* = CALAG.

80. (a) is found in almost all other cases where a Low (Broad) Vowel is final or next to the final consonant. Final *e* is almost always sounded (a).

81. E is found in most syllables of which the letter *i* is that which is next to the final consonants *l*, *n*, *r*, *y*, and *d*, with exceptions which come under the next group. It is found also in the syllables *ear* (meaning Agency), and *ean* (meaning Diminutiveness), as, *muillear* = MULLER ; *cuilean* = CULEN.

82. I and (i) are used indiscriminately in words of which the following are typical, *maighstir*, *tobair*, *astair*; *bodaich*, *bòidhich*; *barraibh*; *gluasaid*, *gilid*; *rachainn*; *uasail*; *umhail*; *milis*; *buailibh*—most of which represent inflected words, i.e. words with something added to convey the sense in which they are used. But it is always I in the Future Tense of Verbs, as, *millidh*, *buailidh*, *togaidh*; in Collective Nouns, as, *òigridh* and, in fact, in most words ending in *idh*.

83. **Consonants in Unaccented Syllables.**—Final *c*, *t*, and *p* of Unaccented Syllables are mostly sounded as if they were *g*, *d*, and *b*.

84. **Provincialisms in Pronunciation.**—The people of different parts of the country have different ways of pronouncing the same words, and they very often write them as they speak them. For instance, the word *beul*, meaning "mouth," is pronounced in some places, BEELL,

and in others, BIaLL. This practice is not confined to one word, but is true of many words which have *eu* and *iu* in the spelling. In some parts, words such as *tom, àm, toll, call, tonn, gann*, have their vowels sounded as if they were diphthongs with W as the second element, thus, TVWM, AWM, TVWLL, CAWLL, TVWNN, GAWNN. In other districts the letter *a* adjoining a Nasal Consonant is pronounced E, as *math* = ME; *àm* = EM; *ann* = ENN; *thàinig* = ·EENiG.

SECTION II.

Words in Composition.

85. Composition.—The term "composition," in ordinary speech, means the putting together of words to express thought. But the meaning of the term as here employed, is the using of a number of words in a single run, as it were, for a certain purpose, such as limiting the application of another word, as,

Thuit clach air mo chois chlì. } A stone fell on my left foot.
Fell stone on my foot left.

86. *Air mo chois chlì* is used in a single run, and bears on the word *thuit* as a single whole, and not in detail. The words of the phrase, if isolated, would be *air, mo, cas, clì*. We see by this that certain words which enter into Composition, suffer changes somewhat like those which take place inside of a single word. We find the old word *mater* — Latin for

"mother"—in modern Gaelic as *mathair*, the *t* becoming *th* in the spelling, because it has lost its original firm sound. In like manner, we see the *c* of *cas* and *cli* becoming, in composition, *ch*. Words in Composition influence one another through the mere fact of coming together.

87. **Mechanical Changes of Words.**—Some of the Changes which words undergo in Composition are, like the case of *cas* and *cli* becoming *chas* and *chli*, merely Mechanical, i.e., due to the tendency to make speaking easier and quicker. They are of no man's devising, but have grown up imperceptibly; and, indeed, are in process of growth, although we may not notice it.

88. **Changes due to Inflection.**—*Cas* became *chois* in the above sentence. *A* changed into *oi* because the sense required it, and not because of any mechanical advantage derivable from the change. This is called Inflection, and will be dealt with in another Section.

89. **Aspiration.**—In treating of the Alphabet, we saw that certain letters took *h* after them. The said *h* is indicative of their decay. Very few words begin with an *h* combination when not in composition. In composition, however, most Initial Consonant Sounds are liable to change to those represented by consonant letters with *h* after them. There are certain circumstances which require the consonant to be so changed. In the preceding Gaelic example *chois* follows *mo*, meaning "my." If it had come after *a*, meaning "her," *c* would not have changed, and the sentence would have read as follows:—

Thuit clach air a cois chli.
Fell stone on her foot left.
} A stone fell on her left foot.

90. We see by that fact, that certain words require the change above exemplified, in the word after them. That change is called Aspiration, and we call a consonant after it has been so changed an Aspirated Consonant.

91. Aspiration in the older language seems to have occurred after words ending in vowels. In the modern language, it does so to a certain extent still; but as most of the old final vowels have dropped off, the original cause of aspiration is in most cases, removed, and leaves nothing on which to found a general rule. Now and again, we meet the original cause of aspiration preserved in provincial speech, for instance, *do'n mhàthair* (to the mother), rendered according to the practice of some districts, is *do'na mhàthair*. Aspiration may also be due to causes other than vowel influence.

92. When words unpreceded by others, are aspirated, it proves that there has been an aspirating influence which has dropped into disuse. It can frequently be reinstated from knowledge of the older language, or by reasoning from other facts of the current language. In the example already given, the word *thuit* is aspirated at its beginning, because of a word, *ro*, which used to precede it in the like circumstances.

93. **Words which aspirate those which follow them.** All the circumstances giving rise to Aspiration cannot be set forth here. They must be learned as they arise. But the words of the following list always aspirate the Initial Consonants of those which follow them.

Do, to; *do,* thy; *mo,* my; *a,* his; *de,* of; *mu,* about; *fo,* under; *o* or *bho,* from; *roimh,* before; *troimh,* through; *mar,* as, like; *glé,* very; *ro,* rather; *dà,* two; *a* (contraction for *do* and *de*), to, of; *an ceud,* the first; *a* (a word placed before the name of anything addressed by name, as, *A Dhòmhnuill,* O, Donald!)

WORDS IN COMPOSITION.

94. The following words aspirate all Aspirable Letters, except *t* and *d*.

Aon, one; *gun*, without; *cha*, not; *bu*, was, were.

95. The following words are always Aspirated when naturally they are expected to be in the Unaspirated form.

Thig, come; *thoir*, give; *their*, will say; *theid*, will go; *bheir*, will give; *gheibh*, will get; *bho*, from; *bhur*, your; *thar* and *thairis*, over, across.

96. The following words are Aspirated and Unaspirated without any seeming regard to rule.

Féin, fhéin, self; *fathast, fhathast*, yet; *tu, thu*, thou; *tà, thà*, is; *domh, dhomh; duit, dhuit*, etc., to me, to you, etc.; *diom, dhìom; dìot, dhìot*, etc., of me, of you, etc.

97. The following words do not aspirate in circumstances where aspiration in the case of other similar words takes place.

So, this; *sin*, that; *sud*, yonder, yon.

98. Words beginning with *sg*, *st*, *sp*, and *sm* cannot aspirate. Those beginning with *sl*, *sr*, and *sn*, aspirate like words with initial *s* before vowels.

99. **Eclipsis.**—Eclipsis means the suppression of a Weak Consonant at the beginning of a word, after an Unaccented Syllable ending in a Nasal Consonant. The name is also applied to the Weakening of a Strong Consonant in the like circumstances. In Scottish Gaelic, it is regarded as a bad usage which is more or less confined to certain districts, but not practised to an extent which justifies grammatical recognition. In the Irish, Manx, and Welsh languages, Eclipsis is a recognised and established grammatical fact which cannot be ignored,

because it is universal. The following are examples of Eclipsis in Scottish Gaelic :—

Tìr nam beann, when pronounced *tir nam eann*.
Gogadh nan ceann, when pronounced *gogadh nan geann*.
Bàrr nan tonn, when pronounced *bàrr nan donn*.
Moch an dé, when pronounced *moch an é*.
An do ghabh thu e, when pronounced *na ghabh thu e*.

100. The preceding are examples in which Eclipsis has only a Partial hold on the language, being kept in check by the firmer pronunciation which maintains in other districts and in literature.

101. The following are examples of cases in which Eclipsis has become established, though not recognisable as such without knowledge of the older literature as it is interpreted by learned students :—

Am bheil, in which a former *f* is softened to *bh* through the influence of a preceding *m*. The words might have been written as they are still pronounced in some parts, *am feil*. In other parts, the words are pronounced *a' bheil;* and this spelling appears very frequently in literature.

Am màireach, in which a former *b* is suppressed through the influence of a preceding *m*, the words having once been, *am bàireach*.

Gu ma, in which a former *b* is suppressed through the influence of a preceding *m*, the words having once been, *gu'm ba* (or *badh*).

102. **Synthesis.**—When two or more Unaccented Words come together and by their presence, drive the Accents wide apart, the tendency is to blend them together, so as to have a Shorter Unaccented Interval. The Gaelic Language may be said to abhor the accents more than three syllables apart. The fusion of words for this purpose is called Synthesis. The occurrence of unaccented words at the beginning of a statement is also distasteful.

Words which coalesce with each other, are written close together, and a sign called the Apostrophe, put in the place of the part left out. The parts of words so left out, are sometimes difficult to reinstate, and require knowledge of the older language ; but in most cases, the reinstatement is easily done.

103. Words ending in Vowels before words beginning in Vowels, are most liable to Synthesis, as, *do'n* for *do an*, *d'iarr* for *do iarr*, *d'fhaod* for *do fhaod*, *m'òglach* for *mo òglach*, *b'fhèarr* for *bu fhèarr*.

104. In some cases, words ending or beginning with consonants, coalesce with others, as, *'nan* for *ann an*, *'nad* for *ann ad*, *ri d'* for *ri do*, *'san* for *anns an*, *'gan* for *ag an*, *'nuair* for *an uair*, *'s tric* for *is tric*.

105. In some cases, as many as three words are blended into one syllable, as, *gu'm b'éiginn* for *gu am bu éiginn*, *gu'n d'fhalbh* for *gu an do fhalbh*.

106. It is quite evident that many of the more commonly used words have come to their present forms through Synthesis. Their elements are not always recognisable. Some may be got at by the study of the older language ; and some suggest their elements in their meaning, as, *agam* for *ag mi*, at me ; *leam* for *le mi*, with me, etc.

107. **Grades of Composition.**—Composition may be regarded as of Three Grades, namely :—

108. LOOSE COMPOSITION, exemplified by *air mo chois chlì*, where the words influence one another without absorbing parts of each other.

109. CLOSE COMPOSITION, exemplified by combinations like *do'n*, *b'fhèarr*, *'san*, etc., where the words are absorbed by one another in such a way that the parts lost may be indicated by an Apostrophe.

110. PERFECT COMPOSITION, exemplified by words like *leam, rium*, etc., where the words are absorbed into one another in such a way that they cannot be separated in the Spelling.

111. **Euphony.**—Some words have developed more than one form owing to the tendency to make speaking easy and fluent, e.g.—

112. *An* becomes *am* before Labial Consonants, as, *am buille*, but *an duine*.

113. *An* drops *n* before Aspirated Letters, as, *air a' chù*, but *air an uisge*. Some drop *n* before *s*, as, *anns a' sgoil;* but this is not the literary usage.

114. *Ag* drops *g* before Consonants, as, *a' bualadh*, but *ag òl*. *Ag radh* is an exception to the rule.

115. *Do* becomes *a*, as, *tha e a' dol a* (*do*) *dhèanamh sin; am fear a* (*do*) *sheinn an t-òran*.

116. *Do* becomes *dh'* before Vowels and *fh*, as, *dh' iarr, dh' fhan*, but *do thuit*.

117. *Do* has its place taken by *ad*, as, *ann ad làimh*, but *air do cheann*.

118. *Mo* has its place taken by *am*, as, *ann am làimh*, but *air mo cheann*.

119. *Ar* and *ur* preserve an *n* before Vowels, as, *ar n-athair, ur n-athair*, but *ar màthair, ur bràthair*. The *n* belonged formerly to the words *ar* and *ur* and was dropped before Consonants.

120. *An* preserves a *t* before Vowels and *s* in certain circumstances which will be dealt with further on, as, *an t-am, air an t-saoghal*. The *t* belonged formerly to the word *an*, and was dropped in all other circumstances.

121. *Air* or *ar* preserves an *n* before Vowels in two instances only, namely, *uidh air n-uidh*, and *an là ar n-a' mhàireach*. The *n* belonged formerly to the word *air* or *ar*, and was dropped in all cases but the two given. In the other Gaelic dialects, evidence of a former *n* is left in the Eclipsis which follows *air* or *ar*.

122. **Reduplication.**—The word *ann* is repeated in certain cases which are not easily defined, as *ann an tigh* (in a house). *Ann* and *an* are forms of the same word, and mean "in."

123. **False Analogy.**—At the beginning of a sentence it is right to say *thuit mi* (I fell), and *dh' iarr mi* (I sought). *Dh' iarr* is assumed to correspond with *thuit:* that is the Analogy. But reference to ¶¶ 92 and 116 will show it to be False, and that *dh' iarr* corresponds to (*do*) *thuit*. The results of this False Analogy are seen in the following words:—

An là air an *do thuit* mi.   The day on which I fell.
An là air an *do dh' iarr* mi e.   The day on which I sought it.

124. False Analogy has given rise to the Reduplication of *do* in the second sentence, which would be better rendered thus, *An là air an d' iarr mi e.* Analogy, as we see, is apt to lead into error. But in language, established errors are not to be regarded as errors. Custom is everything. Yet, when more than one custom prevails, it is sometimes possible to supersede that which knowledge shows to be wrong, by that which is right.

125. **Words Confounded with One Another.**—*Do* (to), and *de* (of), are much confounded the one with the other, and it is sometimes difficult to say when it is *do*, or when it is *de*, which was formerly used. Both break down to *a*, and both suffer Reduplication arising from False Analogy, as in the following words:—

Tha mi a' dol do dh' (a dh') Eirinn.   I am going to Ireland.
Armailt mhòr de dh' (a dh') eich.   A great army of horses.

126. It is not incorrect to say *do Eirinn, de eich*, but the Hiatus is found inconvenient. Hence we find *a dh'* most frequently used before Vowels for *do* and *de*.

127. **Elision of Syllables.**—When a word of more than one syllable, ending in a Vowel, precedes another beginning with a Vowel, it is a common practice to drop one of the Vowels, either to avoid hiatus or to bring the accents closer, as *gill' òg* for *gille òg; duin' uasal* for *duine uasal; Coir'-a'-cheathaich* for *Coire a' cheathaich*.

128. **Elision of Words.**—A Word is frequently left out altogether when Aspiration, or the Order of the Words, reveals its absence, or when the Sense of the Words used suggests the absent word. This takes place chiefly when the dropt word is a Single Vowel, and would follow, if used, a Final Vowel in the preceding word, as, *Tha mi 'dol* for *tha mi a' (ag) dol; Chuir e 'bhoineid air 'cheann* for *chuir e a bhoineid air a cheann; Cha do sheinn Calum 'òran* for *Cha do sheinn Calum a òran*. The word *a* (his) is scarcely ever used before a vowel. As has already been noticed, *do* is rarely ever used at the beginning of a sentence, as, *thuit clach* for *do thuit clach*, except before words beginning with a vowel; and then it becomes *dh'*, as *dh' iarr mi deoch*.

129. **Words Similarly Pronounced.**—Words Similarly Pronounced are known by the Context, or by the Modulations of the Voice, in Speaking. In Writing, there is frequently some helping mark, as, *gun* and *gu'n; nan* and *na'n* or *'nan; ma* and *m'a; 'na* and *na*, etc.

SECTION III.

Words in Regard to their Formation and Development.

130. **Derivation.**—Derivation is the term applied to the tracing back of words to earlier forms, for the purpose of showing how their growth proceeded; but in ordinary grammar, it is commonly applied to the tracing of words to the Simplest Forms in Current Use, and it is not usual to go beyond this, except by way of illustration.

131. **Primitive Words.**—Words from which others are built, are called Primitive Words. A Primitive Word is one which is not derived from another known word in current use.

132. **Derivative Words.**—Derivative Words are those which are formed from Primitive Words by the addition of a syllable, or syllables, to the end, as,

> Prim. Sona—happy, Der. Sonas—happiness;
> Prim. Fear—man, Der. Fearail—manly.

133. **Compound Words.**—New words are formed by placing certain words which suggest the new idea, side by side. They enter into Loose Composition, and are called Compound Words. The parts of a compound word are always separated by a Hyphen in writing, and the Accent, as a rule, follows the hyphen, as,

> Ard-easbuig—archbishop; Saor-thoil—free-will.*

---

* The second parts of Compound Words are subject to Aspiration in circumstances the explanation of which must be reserved for a more advanced stage.

134. Prefixes.—In the case of many compound words, the syllables which go first have no part in speech as separate words, but are used only to change the character of those words before which they are placed. They are called Prefixes, and enter into Loose Composition with the word which they precede, as,

Mì-rùn—ill-will; Neo-iomchuidh—unfit; Di-mol—dispraise.

135. Suffixes.—Syllables placed at the ends of words are called Suffixes, as,

Sona, son*as*; Fear, fear*ail*; Treun, treun*mhor*.

136. Affixes.—Prefixes and Suffixes are included in the more general term Affix, which may mean syllables added at either end.

137. Advance of the Accent.—Compound Words are liable to have the Accent transferred to the first part. When that has taken place, the word is no longer to be regarded as Compound, but as Derivative, and the hyphen must no longer be used. For instance, *comh-dhàil* has become *còmhdhail*; *sean-fhacal*, *seanfhacal*. The words have entered into Close Composition.

138. When a Compound Word is found which has the accent sometimes on the Second and sometimes on the First element, it may be said to be Transitional, i.e., in process of changing from a Compound to a Derivative. For instance, *comh-thional* and *coimhthional*; *neò-dhuine* and *neòdhuine*; *mì-chiat* and *mìchiat*.

139. Words of this kind when they are written to represent the accent on the First part, have sometimes to have the spelling adjusted to suit the rule. For instance, *mì-rùn* has to be written *mìorun*, *mì thlachd*, *mìothlachd*; *an-fhiach*, *ainfhiach*; *cas-bheart*, *caisbheart*.

140. A few words of this class have not been written conform to rule, as, *neoni* for *neoini, lethbhodach* for *leabhodach*.

141. **Syncope.**—Words are constantly progressing from Compound to Derivative, and from Derivative to Primitive forms. After compounds have reached the Derivative Stage, they often proceed by way of blending the Unaccented Syllables with one another, or with the Accented one. This is called Syncope. For instance, *ubhal + an*, syncopated to *ùbhlan; foghainn + idh*, to *foghnuidh; sleamhainn + achd*, to *sleamhnachd; socair + ich*, to *socraich; truagh + as*, to *truas; latha*, to *là; bitheadh*, to *biodh*.

142. The following are examples of Syncope having taken place along with Advance of the Accent :—*mì-mhodhail*, syncopated to *mìomhail; cas-bheart*, to *caiseart; iom-chubhaidh*, to *iomchuidh*.

143. Syncope may have taken place in speaking, long before it is acknowledged in writing, as, *cùlthaobh*, when it is pronounced *cùlaobh; caisbheart*, when it is pronounced *caiseart*.

144. When two Short syllables, one of which is the Accented one, have been blended into one, that one is a Long syllable, as, *latha, là; comhair, còir; leotha, leò; riutha, riù; rithis, rìs*. This rule does not hold in the case of some words of very frequent use, as, *bitheadh, biodh; tabhair, toir;* which have not only suffered Syncope, but tend also to lose the Accent.

SECTION IV.

Words in Regard to the Functions they Fulfil in the Expression of Thought.

145. **Sentences.**—Complete thoughts expressed in words are called Sentences.

146. **Nouns.**—Before we can think, we must have something to think about; and, before we can express our thoughts, we must have a Name for that something. Name words are called Nouns.

147. **Verbs.**—We must also have a word, or words, to tell what we think about that thing. Tell-words are called Verbs.

148. **Subject and Predicate.**—It often happens that one word is not sufficient to tell what we think about, or what we think about it, so we have recourse to other words to help us. But, no matter how many words we use, that which we think about is called the Subject, and that which we think about the Subject is called the Predicate.

149. **Person.**—Every expression of thought presupposes a speaker, who may speak for himself alone, or for himself along with others, and also a person, or persons, spoken to. The person who speaks, is called the First Person; and the word he uses to speak of himself, or of himself along with others, is said to be in the First Person. The word used for the person, or persons, spoken to, is said to be in the Second Person. That used for the thing about which the averment is made—in fact every word which is not in the first or second person—is said to be in the Third Person.

150. **Limitation.**—If a Name-word, or Noun, is applied to one object only, we call it a Particular Term, e.g. *Muile* (Mull). If it can be applied to more than one object, it is called a General Term, e.g. *clach* (a stone). But, for the purposes of language, no word in itself is regarded as a Particular Term ; for we can say *Tha ioma Muile ann* (There are many Mulls), thus using *Muile* as a General Term applicable to more than one object. All nouns are therefore assumed to be General, and before they can be reduced to the nature of Particular Terms, they have to be Limited by the addition of other words. Some words admit of a more general application than others. For instance, *tuit* (fall) can be said of any material thing ; but *clach* (a stone) is limited to a certain kind of things, for any other material cannot be called *clach*. *Tuit* is a Tell-word, or Verb ; *clach* is a Name-word or Noun. Of the two essentials of a sentence—the Noun and the Verb—the Verb is the more General.

151. **The Order of the Noun and Verb.**—It is the practice of the Gaelic Language to put the more General Term, or Verb, first, and limit its application by the Noun. This practice gives a distinct advantage to the Gaelic Language over many others which put the Noun first.*

152. Take the following sentence as an example :—

Thuit clach. } A stone fell.
Fell stone.

153. *Thuit* makes an averment. *Clach* tells us what it is about. *Thuit* might be affirmed of almost anything. *Clach* limits its application to a certain kind of thing.

* See Herbert Spencer's *Essay on Style.*

154. Tense.—*Thuit*, it will be noticed, begins with an Aspirated Consonant. When a verb in its simple form, at the Beginning of a Sentence, begins with an Aspirated Consonant, it is, as a rule, in the Past Tense, i.e., it refers to a past time or a completed action. The reason for the aspiration of *tuit* to represent the past tense was given at ¶ 92. To make a verb refer to a time to come requires it to be inflected. This is done by adding a suffix, *idh* or *aidh*, to the primitive form. A verb referring to a time to come, is said to be in the Future Tense. *Tuitidh* is the Future Tense of *tuit*; *togaidh* of *tog*. Only a few verbs express Present Tense. One of them is *tha*. But it, like *thuit*, is aspirated, showing the influence of a word which goes before it in circumstances other than the beginning of a sentence.

155. Exercise. Translate the following sentences into English :—

Bhuail fear. Choisich gille. Fhreagair caileag. Shéid gaoth. Chinn feur. Bhàsaich cù. Sheinn balach. Ghairm coileach. Chaolu pàisde. Ghàir bodach. Leum iasg. Mhèilich uan. Gheum bò. Shuidh cailleach. Bhruidhinn bean. Loisg maide. Theich fiadh. Sheas each. Tuitidh craobh. Bhris botul. Seinnidh eun. Shil fras. Leumaidh sionnach. Thòisich sabaid. Chaidil leanabh. Leanaidh iasgair. Ghuil bean. Sheòl bàta. Loisgidh fiodh. Dhùisg caileag. Gearraidh sgian. Fàsaidh bàrr. Sheirm clag. Mairidh ceòl. Chlisg giullan. Seargaidh duilleag.

156. Adjectives.—All other words which are used in Simple Sentences, are for limiting the Verb or the Noun. The following sentence illustrates a word limiting a Noun :—

Thuit clach bheag.} A small stone fell.
Fell stone small.

157. *Cluch* is limited as to size, by the word *bheag*, i.e., it is described. *Bheag* belongs to a class of Descriptive Words called Adjectives.

158. **Composition.**—*Clach bheag* together limit *thuit*, and are said to enter into Composition. The Adjective enters into Loose Composition with its Noun. *Bheag* begins with an aspirated consonant after *clach*. After certain Nouns it would not aspirate, as, *duine beag* (a little man). *Duine* belongs to a class of Nouns which are followed by Unaspirated Adjectives. *Clach* belongs to a class of Nouns which are followed by Aspirated Adjectives. So we see that words which enter into Composition, not only influence each other, but influence each other differently.

159. **Gender.**—When a Noun limiting a Verb, requires an Unaspirated Adjective after it, it is said to be of the Masculine Gender. When the Adjective is Aspirated, the Noun is of the Feminine Gender. All the changes which Nouns of the Masculine Gender undergo in Composition, are distinctly different from those which Nouns of the Feminine Gender undergo. It is by these differences we know when a Noun is Masculine or Feminine, and not by the sex of the actual object of which the Noun is the Name. At the same time, most Names of Male objects are of the Masculine Gender, and those of Female objects, mostly of the Feminine Gender. "Gender" is, therefore, merely a grammatical term enabling us to speak of nouns in two classes, differing from each other in their inflections and their effects on accompanying words.* Unlike the English and some

---

* With this as the definition of "Gender," English grammar might dispense with the term.

other languages, which have three genders, the Gaelic has only two.

160. The Order of the Noun and Adjective.—As a rule, the Adjective follows the Noun. Sometimes the Adjective is put before the Noun to give it prominence, as *binn cheòl*. But when that is done, the words together are of the nature of a Compound, and, if often used, are subject to the same influences as Compound Words.

161. Adjectives are of more general application than Nouns; and putting the more general term after the less general, seems the reverse of the economical order. But there is a good reason for this. If we were to introduce the Adjective first, we would have to carry on our minds two unlimited terms before the Noun came in to limit both, whereas, by introducing the Noun before the Adjective, the limitation of the verb is completed, and only one unlimited term is on the mind at a time. If, like the English practice, the Noun came before the Verb, it would be right to put the Adjective first and limit its application by the Noun. But the English practice is not as good as the Gaelic practice, which puts the tell-word first, and makes compensation for the position of the Adjective, by Accent, as will be shown further on.

162. An adjective may come after a noun without entering into Composition with it. When it does so, it is said, or predicated, of the Noun; and the Verb used then, merely asserts, without implying action, and belongs to a certain class to be afterwards defined. For example:—

Tha feur glas. } Grass is green.
Is grass green. }

THE FUNCTIONS OF WORDS. 39

163. EXERCISE. Translate the following sentences into English :—

Bhuail fear mór. Ruith each bàn. Shnàmh tunnag riabhach. Leum iasg beag. Chaochail tuathanach beairteach. Throd cailleach chrosda. Shiubhail duin' òg. Thuit tigh àrd. Chinn càl math. Theich caora mhaol. Shil fras throm. Phòs nighean bhòidheach. Tha uan beag. Tha teine dearg. Tha sneachd geal. Sheinn ribhinn òg. Labhair duine còir. Tha iarunn cruaidh. Ghuil leanabh òg. Tha ceòl binn. Tha aran feumail. Bhris soitheach beag. Theich abhag dhonn. Bhàsaich cuilean beag. Chinn feur uaine. Seòlaidh long mhór. Leum duine borb. Tha radan bradach. Tha piseag faoin. Ruith cù luath. Tha bainne geal. Caidlidh leanabh math. Ghàir bean mhór. Stad each mall. Tha meas pailte. Tha gual dubh. Tha òr trom. Bhàsaich muc reamhar. Tha sionnach seòlta. Tha dearcag milis. Ghèarr sgian gheur. Shèap cat glas.

164. **Limitation of Noun by Noun.**—One Noun is often used to limit another. When a Noun does so, it is assumed to have begotten, or to have property in, the first mentioned; or it means the same thing as the first. For example :—

Thuit mac Dhòmhnuill. } Donald's son fell.
Fell   son   of-Donald. }

Thuit crioman cloiche. } A bit of stone fell.
Fell   bit   of-stone. }

Thuit Dòmhnull tàillear. } Donald the tailor fell.
Fell   Donald   tailor. }

165. **Case.**—*Dòmhnull* and *clach* are the Uninflected forms of the words meaning "Donald" and "stone." *Dhòmhnuill* and *cloiche* are Inflected forms. The former are said to be in the Nominative Case. The latter are in the Genitive Case. A Noun is in the Nominative Case when it limits a Verb. It is in the Genitive Case when it limits another Noun not meaning the

same thing. In the third example, *Dòmhnull* limits a Verb, and is in the Nominative Case. *Tàillear* limits *Dòmhnull*, but means the same thing. It is, therefore, also in the Nominative Case. It is said to be in Apposition to *Dòmhnull*. Nouns have other cases, which will be referred to further on. A Noun and its Limiting Noun enter into Loose Composition.

166. **Proper Nouns and Common Nouns.**—It will be noticed that *Dhòmhnuill* in the first example, begins with an Aspirated Consonant. *Dòmhnull* is a person's name. Donald can claim the name as his own. The names of persons and places are called Proper Nouns. All others are called Common. Names given to individual objects to single them out from others of the same class, is a better definition of Proper Nouns. As a rule, with some exceptions, Masculine Proper Names are Aspirated in the Genitive Case. Not so Feminine Proper Names: they remain Unaspirated in the Genitive. Numerous instances of Feminine Proper Names following the analogy of Masculine Nouns and aspirating in the Genitive, might be given, nevertheless, from the colloquial speech of certain districts. But even for such colloquial speech, it would be difficult to formulate a rule. Almost all Grammarians have preferred to regard aspiration of Feminine Proper Nouns in the Genitive, as a breach of rule.*

167. EXERCISE. Translate the following sentences into English:—

Thill mac Móraig. Phòs nighean Thormaid. Shiubhail Calum buachaille. Loisg crioman maide. Dhùin dorus taighe. Bhris

* It is often the case also, in colloquial speech, that, when a Proper Noun and an Adjective are used together as a distinctive appellation, the Adjective is uninflected for the Genitive, as, *Boineid Anna bheag* (Little Annie's bonnet), not *Boineid Anna bhig* according to literary usage.

THE FUNCTIONS OF WORDS. 41

geug craoibhe. Shrac Seumas duilleag leabhair. Ghèarr Alasdair corrag Eachainn. Leum cù Eanraig sruth uisge. Chaochail bean Dheòrsa. Tha cuilean Dhòmhnuill leisg. Sheinn Ceit bheag. Leughaidh duine còir. Bhàsaich cat dubh Cairistìona òig. Tha bean Dhonnachaidh crosda. Tha othaisg Sheumais bhochd marbh. Theich cù Dhòmhnuill mhóir. Thàinig each bàn Lachainn. Tha làir dhonn Dhùghaill chrùbaich làidir. Phòs mac Uilleim. Sgrìobh giullan òg. Tha Griogair mór bodhar. Dhùisg pàisde beag Marsali. Tha mart mhaol Eanraig sean. Thill Seumas ciobair. Sheinn Calum greusaiche. Throd seanmhair Iseabail. Ghàir gille fada caol. Dhanns caileag bheag, sgiobalta. Shuidh Anna dhonn. Eiridh stoirm uamhasach. Tuitidh craobh àrd. Tha madadh mór Iain ruaidh colgarra.

168. **Prepositions.** — The Adjective and the Noun, as we have seen, can be used to Complete a Limitation. We now come to a class of words which cannot be so used. No sentence can end in a Preposition. It is a word of very general application, and is used in its Primary Sense to express Relation in Space. But it can be applied to express almost any kind of relation. For an example of the preposition:—

Thuit clach air cloich. } A stone fell on a stone.
Fell stone on stone.

Thuit clach air Calum. } A stone fell on Calum.
Fell stone on Calum.

169. *Air cloich* and *air Calum* together limit *thuit* by telling the place on which the stone fell. *Thuit air cloich* is the Predicate, and, as we see, it is divided. It is admissible to say *thuit air cloich clach* when we wish to give prominence to *air cloich*, but it is not often that is wanted. *Air* and *cloich* enter into Loose Composition. *Cloich* is an Inflected form of *clach* owing to the Preposition preceding it. It is in the Dative Case.

42 GAELIC GRAMMAR.

A Preposition enters into Composition with its Noun, and is said to govern it in the Dative Case. *Calum* shows no change from its Nominative form, although preceded by a preposition. Nevertheless, it is also said to be in the Dative Case; for it is not from the facts belonging to one noun, but from those which belong to nouns in the aggregate, that the number and names of cases are determined.

170. Prepositions are limited in number, and the following is a list of those most frequently in use, given along with their primary meanings. The forms in brackets are less common variations, reference to which will be made at a future stage.

171.   PREPOSITIONS.

Air (ar), on, upon.   Fo (fuidh), under.
Aig (ag), at.   Gu (gus), to.
An (am, ¶ 111, ann, ann an,   Le (leis), with, along with, by.
  ¶ 122, anns), in, into.   Mu, about.
As (á), out of.   O (bho, uaidh, bhuaidh), from,
De (a, a dh', de dh', ¶ 125),   since.
  of, off.   Ri (ris), towards, to.
Do (a, a dh', do dh', ¶ 125), to. Roimh (romh), before.
Eadar, between.   Thar, over, across.
    Troimh (tromh, tre, trid), through.

172. EXERCISE. Translate the following sentences into English :—

Tha sionnach air cnoc. Tha bàta air loch. Sheas cù air lic. Leum gabhar air creig. Bhruidhinn Seònaid mu Shìne. Tha leabhar an laimh Mòir. Chaidh luchag an toll. Bithidh cat air cathair. Theid each le Dùghall. Thàinig caraid do thigh Fionnghaill. Tillidh mac Eachainn do bhaile Ghlascho. Théid Ealasaid gu banais Màiri. Chaochail Iain air Di-luain. Leum Iain air tìr. Thill Peigi do thigh Dhòmhnuill òig. Thuit clach an amhainn. Thàinig gille gu Caisteal Tiorram. Chaidh luch

fo chloich. Théid each thar drochaid. Thàinig Pàdruig troimh
chruadal. Labhair duine ri Màiri. Thuit creag le fuaim mhóir.
Theich cù á tigh Thormaid. Chaidh sluagh mór dh' America.
Tha astar fada o cheann gu ceann Loch Odha. Ruith Eachann
mu ghàradh Iain ruaidh. Chaidh long bhrèagha fo sheòl.
Thàinig bàta gu cladach. Tha crioman beag iaruinn fo chloich
bhig. Teichidh Calum roimh Sheumas. Sguir Alasdair mu
fheasgar. Chlisg giullan beag le h-eagal.

173. **Limitation by Circumstance.**—In the sentence, *Thuit clach air Calum*, Calum is a person's name. But it is a common name. How do we know to whom it applies ? If we were talking together and giving utterance to the preceding sentence, we would use the word *Calum* so, only if it were perfectly well understood which Calum was meant. If that were not understood, we would have to use words limiting the application of the word *Calum*. But when we know which Calum it is, without any limiting words, to use such words would be superfluous, and language abhors superfluous words. We speak of the word *Calum* as being limited by Circumstance. The Calum referred to might be the Calum of whom we were previously speaking, the Calum best known to the company, or of whom it was customary to speak as Calum.

174. An example of a sentence composed of a Verb alone, limited in its application by Circumstance, is that common one in which a command is given, as,

Buail, strike.

175. No mention is made of the speaker; that is always apparent. No mention is made of the person spoken to; that also is generally apparent. Nor of the object to be struck ; that, if not quite apparent from the words, may be otherwise indicated. But in the above

sentence, every necessary limitation is understood, or assumed by the speaker to be understood. If the speaker is wrong in his assumption, he will have to repeat the sentence with all the limitations expressed, and then the sentence may take this form :—

>Buail Dùghall, a Chaluim.
>Strike Dugald, Calum.

176. If Calum were inattentive, it might be necessary to alter the order of the words by saying the name of the person addressed first, as,

>A Chaluim, buail Dùghall.
>Calum, strike Dugald.

177. **Object.**—*Buail* is a Verb intimating a wish of the speaker, expressed as a command. It is said of the Speaker. Hence there is no limitation by Subject, as the same is unnecessary. The word itself is an indication that the Speaker is the Subject. *Dùghall* is the Object or person to be struck. The Object is a limitation of the Verb or Predicate, and always appears in the Nominative case. *Buail* is a Verb of action, and the action is assumed to pass to, or be spent on, an object. Some Verbs do not express action which can be assumed to be spent on an object, as, *caidil* (sleep). Those Verbs which have an object, are called Transitive. Those which have none, are called Intransitive. There is besides these classes, another class which do not express action at all, as, *bì* (be). They are called Substantive.

178. **Vocative Case.**—It will be noticed that *Calum*, in the sentence, *Buail Dùghall, a Chaluim*, is inflected. When a Noun is the name of a person or thing spoken to, it is in the Vocative Case.

THE FUNCTIONS OF WORDS. 45

179. **Vocative Particle.**—The word *a* which precedes *Chaluim* has no meaning whatever. It is used because it is the practice to use it before Nouns in the Vocative Case. There is an advantage in retaining it in speech, otherwise it would have gone long since. It serves to draw the attention; for, without the warning *a*, the name following it might pass unheeded. The Noun and the Vocative Particle enter into Loose Composition and limit the Verb in regard to Second Person, or person spoken to. The Vocative Particle is left out before vowels, as, *Tog clach*, *'Eachainn* (Lift a stone, Hector).

180. EXERCISE. Translate the following sentences into English:—

Buail dorus, a Chaluim. Eisd ri òran binn Peigi. Bris clach, 'Uilleim. Dùisg, a lunndaire. Gairm air cù Iain. Tog ultach feòir. Ith crioman arain. Ol deoch mhilis. Taom cuinneag Marsali bhig. Lion botul le uisge. Dheasaich Màiri bonnach do Raonull. Bha còta beag air mac òg Lachainn ruaidh. 'Alasdair, tionndaidh ri Pòl. Iomair buille, Eòghainn. Glac làmh Choinnich. Teich as rathad Iain mhóir. Rinn Iseabal sgread cruaidh. Thog fear làidir clach mhór, throm. Thug gille tapaidh each bodaich bhochd á boglaich. Ghabh Calum sgliatair deoch uisge. Tha each Mhànuis air theadhair. Cuidich bràthair Màiri, a Shomhairle. A dhuine thruaigh, òl deoch-bhainne. Bha Mór aig banais Cholla. Tha leanabh Ealasaid tinn. Bha Di-màirt blàth. Ith bonnach beag. Gabh crioman càise. Thoir spàin do mhac Lachainn. Innis sgeul do Fhearghus. Ghèarr Iain meanglan de chraoibh àird le tuaigh.

181. **The Article.**—For the explanation of this part of speech take the following sentence:—

Thuit an duine. } The man fell.
Fell the man.   }

182. *An* is called the Article. It always precedes the Noun and enters into Composition with it. If the sentence were *Buail duine*, *duine* would be unlimited,

and might mean any of the species called *duine,* or "man." If we said *Buail an,* it would be altogether unsatisfactory. *An* is one of the vague terms of the language, which are used merely for form's sake. When we add *duine* we limit the application of *an* to a certain thing, the species of which is expressed by *duine.* But here two things have to be considered. *An duine* may mean the human race, or a certain individual of the race. *An* is subject to Limitation by Circumstance, and it is only by using our judgment that we know when it points to an individual person or thing, or when it means the entire species or class.

183. **Antecedent.**—When *an* points back to a word before spoken or a subject understood, it is said to have an Antecedent. For instance :—

| Bha duine aig an dorus an dé. | A man was at the door |
| Was man at the door yesterday. | yesterday. |

| Bha an duine liath. | |
| Was the man grey. | The man was grey-haired. |

184. The *an* in the second sentence points back to the word *duine* in the first sentence, which is called its Antecedent. *An* is therefore limited by the circumstance that it has an Antecedent. *An* before *dorus* is limited by the circumstance that *dorus* is the door which cannot be mistaken—the door of the house belonging to the speaker or the hearer, or some other door equally well understood. The *an* before *dé* is limited by the fact that there is only one yesterday.

185. When *an* is not limited by any preceding words, it can only be limited by the judgment. For instance:—

| Tha an cù math air ruith. | |
| Is the dog good on running. | The dog is good at running. |

186. We cannot say from the above words, whether it is the dog as a species, or a particular dog, which is meant. We must just use our judgment in considering the circumstances in which the words are spoken, or else ask to have an explanation.

187. The Article takes a limited number of forms which are dependent on the nature of the word which follows it.

188. The Article also enters into composition, more or less close, with a preposition preceding it, as,

Thuit clach air an làr. } A stone fell on the ground.
Fell stone on the ground.

Rach mu 'n chloich.   Go round about the stone.

189. *Air an làr* and *mu 'n chloich* limit *thuit* and *rach* respectively.

190. **Adjectives have Case.**—In the following sentence, the Preposition, Article, Noun, and Adjective enter into Composition to limit the Verb :—

Rach mu 'n chloich bhig. } Go round about the small
Go round about the stone small. } stone.

191. *Bhig* is an inflected form of *beag*. It follows *cloich*, which is in the Dative Case. We see by this that Adjectives are, like Nouns, inflected for Case. Adjectives are said to agree with their Nouns in Case.

192. **Number.**—Nouns take different inflections for the expression of Number, and these vary for the expression of Case. Adjectives are subject to corresponding inflections. Nouns signifying more than one thing, are said to be in the Plural Number. Those signifying only one thing, are in the Singular Number. The Adjective agrees with its Noun in Number and Case. It has already been shown to agree with it in Gender.

The following examples show Nouns and Adjectives inflected for Number, Case, and Gender:—

Thuit fir mhóra. } Big men fell.
Fell men big.

Thuit clachan móra. } Big stones fell.
Fell stones big.

193. Inflections of the Article.—The inflections of the Article, owing to the fact that it enters so thoroughly into Composition, are complex, and have to be noted in reference to Gender, Number, Case, and the Letters which it precedes.

SINGULAR.

Before Vowels.

	Nom.	Gen.	Dat.
MASC.	An t-	An	An, 'n
FEM.	An	Na h-	An, 'n

Before c, g.

MASC.	An	A' (ch)	A' (ch), 'n (ch)
FEM.	A' (ch)	Na	A' (ch), 'n (ch)

Before p, b, m.

MASC.	Am	A' (ph)	A' (ph), 'n (ph)
FEM.	A' (ph)	Na	A' (ph), 'n (ph)

Before d, t, l, n, r.

MASC.	An	An	An, 'n
FEM.	An	Na	An, 'n

Before s, sl, sr, sn.

MASC.	An	An t-	An t-, 'n t-
FEM.	An t-	Na	An t-, 'n t-

Before st, sg, sp.

MASC.	An	An	An, 'n
FEM.	An	Na	An, 'n*

* Sometimes the Dative Feminine is *A'* for *An* before *s* (see ¶ 113).

THE FUNCTIONS OF WORDS.

	Nom.	SINGULAR. Before f. Gen.	Dat.
MASC.	Am	An (fh)	An (fh), 'n (fh)
FEM.	An (fh)	Na	An (fh), 'n (fh)

PLURAL.

| MASC. | Na | Nan | Na |
| FEM. | | Nam (before Labials, ¶ 111). | |

194. The letters in brackets are to indicate when the Noun following is Aspirated. Where there are no brackets, the Noun which follows the Article is Unaspirated.

195. In the pronunciation of *s, sl, sn, sr*, after *an t-* or *'n t-*, the Consonant *s* is aspirated although it is not so written. *Air an t-saoghal* is spoken *air-ant-shaoghal*.

196. The prepositions *ann, gu, le*, and *ri* alter their forms before the Article, thus: *anns an,* gus an, leis an, ris an*. In reality these words enter into Perfect Composition and are pronounced *annsan, gusan, leisean, risean*. The *s* originally belonged to the Article, but having decayed in other circumstances, was not recognised as part of the Article in the above combinations. To write *le san, ri san*, would not correctly represent the pronunciation of *s*, which is High (Small) in these two cases.

197. The other Prepositions ending in Vowels enter into Close Composition with the Article, as, *do'n, do'n t-*, for *do an, do an t-*, etc.

---

* *Anns an* must not be confounded with *ann an*. In the former, *an* is the Article; in the latter, *an* is the Preposition reduplicated (¶ 122).

198. EXERCISE. Translate the following sentences into English :—

Eisd ris an òran bhinn.* Chuir Màiri crioman maide air an teine. Thug Anna biadh do 'n duine bhochd. Thoir freagradh caomh do 'n leanabh òg. Fuasgail an t-each as a' chairt, a bhalaich. Tiormaich am bòrd leis a' bhréid, a Ghiorsal. Fosgail an uinneag, a Shilis. Thilg na fir clach mhór anns an amhainn. Splon Donnachadh an sgian gheur á laimh Thormaid bhig. Tha nead an eòin anns a' chraoibh àird. Eirich, a Phàdruig, as do leabaidh bhlàth. Tha na craobhan àrd. Tha geugan nan craobhan fada. Thaom Màiri an t-uisge as a' chuinneig. Tha meanglain mhóra air a' chraoibh dharaich. Choinnich mi Alasdair air an staidhir. Tholl e na brògan leis a' mhinidh. Bha am buachaille anns an t-sabhull mu fheasgar. Dìrich am bruthach, a Cholla, mo rùin. Shuidh an duine an cathair Seònaid. Tha biodag air an fhleasgach òg. Tha an t-àite fuar falamh. Thug Iain beum do Niall leis an t-slait bhig.

199. **Limitation of Noun by Article.**—The Article, itself limited by a Noun, is used to limit a preceding Noun, as,

Thuit mac an tàilleir. } The tailor's son fell.
Fell son of-the tailor.

200. The words *an tàilleir* together limit *mac*. The words *mac an tàilleir* together limit *thuit*, and enter into Loose Composition. The Limitation *tàilleir* may be further limited by an Adjective, as,

Thuit mac an tàilleir bhig. } The little tailor's son fell.†
Fell son of-the tailor little.

---

* Adjectives coming after Nouns in the Dative Case preceded by the Article, are aspirated.

† It must be noted that it is inadmissible to use the Article before a Noun limited by the Article, thus,

Thuit am mac an tàilleir bhig. } The little tailor's son fell.
Fell the son of-the tailor little.

201. EXERCISE. Translate the following sentences into English :—

Thill mac an duine bhig. Bhris bàrr a' chlaidheimh mhòir. Gabh crioman de 'n aran choirce. Fhuair mi blasad beag ime. Tha toiseach a' bhàta ri ceann an loch. Tha deireadh na luinge ris a' chladach. Tha nead an dreathainn duinn anns a' phreas. Tha ceò air mullach a' mhonaidh àird. Tha sneachd am bràigh a' ghlinne. Tha ceòl binn anns an eaglais mhóir. Tha dorsan air na h-eaglaisean. Tha casan fada air a' chòrr. Fàg am baile aig toiseach an t-samhraidh. Tha earball an t-sionnaich dosach. Tha an t-uan an tigh a' chiobair. Tha sgiobair a' bhàta air tir. Tha làmhan nan daoine salach. Thàinig na fir á Tir nam beann. Tha falt na h-òighe fada. Thàinig Rob gu crich na sgeulachd. Leag Murchadh fiadh anns a' ghleann. Reic Fearchar na h-eich. Cheannaich Cailean na leabhraichean beaga do na sgoileirean. Thog Ailean donn na siùil ris a' chrann àrd. Chunnaic mi fiadh anns a' choire. Tha ceòl nan eun taitneach do 'n chluais. Chuala mi fuaim na trombaide.

202. **The Adverbial Particle.**—The Adverbial Particle is *gu*, and it enters into Composition with a Descriptive Word or Adjective to limit a Verb.* For instance :—

Thuit clach gu luath. } A stone fell quickly.
Fell stone quick.

203. *Gu luath* limits *thuit* in regard to speed. *Gu* is a word having to the modern Gael no meaning whatever. It no doubt had at one time a definite meaning. But it

---

* It is usual to name *gle*, *sàr*, *ro*, *fior*, etc., Adverbs when they precede Adjectives. But they are nowise different from Prefixes, except that they are written unattached. That other languages classify certain words which limit Verbs in regard to manner, degree, time, place, etc., as Adverbs, is no reason for the admission of even the term Adverb into the Grammar of the Gaelic Language. An Adjective used with *gu* to limit a Verb suffers no change; no addition is made to it; and *gu* is not a prefix.

serves a useful purpose, and, therefore, survives the loss of its meaning. The above sentence without *gu* has a different meaning.

Thuit clach luath. } A quick stone fell.
Fell stone quick. }

204. *Luath* without *gu* limits *clach*. *Gu* is the word indicating when the Descriptive Word (Adjective) applies to the Predicate (Verb) and not to the Subject (Noun).

205. An Adjective preceded by *gu*, is subject to Limitation by another Adjective, as,

Thuit clach gu math luath. } A stone fell pretty quickly.
Fell stone good quick. }

206. *Gu math* is a very General Limitation, and we could hardly expect it to end a limitation of *thuit*. It is itself finally limited by *luath*, which particularises it.

207. EXERCISE. Translate the following sentences into English :—

Theich na fir gu grad. Bhuail Calum an t-innean gu trom. Sgriobh na cléirich gu luath. Tha an là gu math fuar. Bha an fhras glé throm. Tha na gillean fior làidir. Ceangail an t-snaim gu teann. Bha searmoin a' mhinistir anabarrach ealanta. Labhair an duine math gu glic. Tha 'n sruthan ro thana. Fàsaidh am feur air mullach an taighe. Ghuil an leanabh gu goirt. Rinn Ceit an obair gu grinn. Choisich na daoine gu h-aotrom. Throd a' bhean gu searbh ris a' ghille. Shéid a' ghaoth gu dian. Labhair an duin' uasal gu foghluimte. Tha Aindreas tinn. Bha na gillean aig a' chladh. Tha Iseabal bheag, nighean Phara piobaire, ro thinn. Bha an oidhche gu math dorcha. Bhuail am buachaille am balach le slait gu goirt. Stiùir am bàta gu beul na h-aimhne. Bhris an tuathanach bata air druim an eich bhàin. Tillidh na fiùrain gu dùthaich nan laoch. Theid gillean nam breacan air toiseach nan gaisgeach. Tha creagan àrda an dùthaich nan Gaidheal. Ol deoch as an fhuaran. Tha an t-astar duilich, cruaidh. Thig làithean frasach, dorcha, trom. Tha guth na ribhinn ceòlmhor. Théid bean a' ghreusaiche bho dhorus gu dorus. Tha gruaidh an duine bhochd gu tana, bàn.

208. **Labour-Saving Words.**—Labour-saving words are for the purpose of avoiding repetition, e.g.:—

Thuit clach *agus* bhris *i*. } A stone fell and it broke.
Fell stone and broke it. }

209. **Conjunction.**—*Agus* joins the statements *thuit clach* and *bhris i* together. Words which join are called Conjunctions. Conjunctions are used between two Verbs, or Predicates, to enable one Noun, or Subject, to apply to both, as,

Thuit agus bhris clach. } A stone fell and broke.
Fell and broke stone. }

210. Conjunctions are used between two Subjects, or Nouns, to make one Predicate, or Verb, serve for both, as,

Thuit clach agus maide. } A stone and a stick fell.
Fell stone and stick. }

211. We are enabled by *agus* to avoid saying *Thuit clach; thuit maide*, and *Thuit clach agus bhris a' chlach*.

212. Conjunctions are limited in number, and are named according to their uses.

213. COPULATIVE.—*Agus*, contracted to *'us* and *'s* (sometimes *a's*) = and.

Is is a form which cannot now be differentiated from *agus* or its contractions. That it is not a contraction for *agus* is apparent in old literature; but there is no reason for retaining it any longer in the language. No one pretends to know when he is using *'us* (contraction for *agus*) or *is*. Its abolition would remove the difficulty caused by the form *is* being both a Conjunction and a Verb. The spelling of contracted *agus* as *a's* should be abandoned, because of another *a's* which is not a conjunction.

's is often used for *agus* or *is* between a word ending with a vowel and another beginning with a Vowel or Consonant, as *duine 's bean.* We see by this that it enters into Composition with the words adjoining it.

214. ALTERNATIVE.—*No* (sometimes *neo*)=or, is used to offer a choice of propositions, as,

Tha fear, no bean, aig a' chladach. ⎱ A man, or a woman, is at the
Is man or woman at the shore. ⎰ shore.

Tog, no fàg, e.   Lift, or leave, it.

215. *No* sometimes enters into Composition with Unaccented Words beginning with a Vowel, as,

An tog mi no 'm (am) fàg mi e? Will I lift or leave it?

216. ADVERSATIVE.—*Ach* = but, places one statement in contrast with another, as,

Thuit fear, ach sheas bean. ⎱
Fell man but stood woman. ⎰ A man fell, but a woman stood.

217. CAUSATIVE.—*Oir* = for, introduces a cause or reason, as,

Gabh do dhinneir oir tha i deas. ⎱ Take your dinner for it
Take your dinner for is it ready. ⎰ is ready.

218. When an Adjective is used to limit two Nouns joined by a Conjunction, it enters into Composition with the one next to it, as if the other were not there, as,

Thuit fear agus bean bhochd. ⎱
Fell man and woman poor. ⎰ A poor man and woman fell.

219. *Bhochd*, as we can see from the Aspiration, agrees with *bean*, Feminine, in preference to *fear*, Masculine.

220. EXERCISE. Translate the following sentences into English :—

Tha fear anns an achadh le each agus cairt. Cuir boineid 'us cleòca air Anna bhig. Tha 'n t-each sean, ach tha e làidir. Rach as an rathad, oir tha thu glé dhraghail. Innis sgeul, no seinn òran. Rach do 'n tigh agus faigh sgian. Dùin an dorus agus fosgail uinneag. Tha mac agus nighean Iain anns an sgoil. Gabhaidh Calum im no càise. Théid Alasdair do 'n bhaile agus fanaidh Cairistìona òg aig an tigh. Tha mnathan 'us clann bheag aig an t-sruth. Tha an t-each bàn agus an làir dhonn anns an achadh, ach tha na laoigh aig taobh an t-sruith. Ni amadan tàir air gliocas agus air teagasg. A mhic, éisd ri teagasg t' athar agus na diùlt comhairle do mhàthar. Faigh an sgian gu luath agus gèarr an ròpa. Tha Iain aig an tigh, ach tha Seumas aig a' chladach leis an làir bhàin. Pillidh freagradh min corruich, ach dùisgidh briathran garga fearg. Bha 'n là fuar, fliuch, agus bha móran de dhaoine bochda mu 'n dorus. Dìon bhur dùthaich 'us cliù bhur sinnsir.

221. Pronouns.—Pronouns, like Conjunctions, are Labour-Saving Words, inasmuch as they save repetition, and one was given as an example at ¶ 208, namely :—

> Thuit clach agus bhris í. } A stone fell and broke.
> Fell stone and broke it. }

222. *I* is a Pronoun, and saves us from saying *thuit clach agus bhris a' chlach*. It points back like the Article *a'* in the last sentence, to some word which goes before it. In this respect, there is an affinity between the Pronoun and the Article. In general, pronouns are words used in place of Antecedent Nouns, but not always; they have other uses, as will be seen.

223. **Personal Pronouns.**—There are seven Pronouns which correspond to *i*, called Personal Pronouns, namely :—

Mi = I and me, used by a speaker to designate himself, or the First Person.

Tu (*thu*) = you, ye, thou and thee, used to designate the person spoken to, or the Second Person.

E (*sè*) = he, it, and him, used to refer to anything not of the First or Second Person, i.e. of the Third Person, when it is of the Male Sex, or is a Masculine Noun.

I (*si*) = she, it, and her, used like *è*, but for Females or Feminine Nouns.

Sinn = we and us, used when the speaker includes others along with him or herself, in the First Person Plural.

Sibh = you and ye, used to designate persons or things in the Second Person Plural of either gender. *Sibh* is used as a mark of respect, particularly to the aged, in place of *thu*.

Iad = they and them, used to refer to any Male or Female, or to Nouns of the Masculine or Feminine Gender, in the Third Person Plural.

224. Some of the Pronouns are in all circumstances Definite, as *mi* and *tu*. Nobody can be called *mi* but the speaker. Nobody can be called *tu* but the person addressed. *Sinn* and *sibh* are not so definite. They are Limited by Circumstance, and we have to use our judgment in knowing who are included in the words. *E*, *i*, and *iad* are Limited by Circumstance always. In general, they refer to an antecedent; but *è* and *iad* are often used formally with no meaning at all, as,

Tha e fliuch an diugh. } It is wet to-day.
Is it wet the day. }

Mar a their iad. } As they say.
As say they. } As the saying is.

225. *E* and *iad*, having no Antecedent in the foregoing sentences, mean nobody in particular. Their purpose is to enable the speaker to carry out the forms of speech. If an Antecedent be introduced, meaning is thereby given to the words *è* and *iad*, as,

Bha Mànus aig an tobar; tha e fliuch. } Magnus was at the well;
Was Magnus at the well; is he wet. } he is wet.

Faic na daoine; tha iad fliuch. } See the men; they are wet.
See the men; are they wet. }

226. *E* now means *Mànus*. *Iad* means *na daoine*. This, again, shows the affinity between the Pronoun and the Article. Without Antecedents or Limiting Circumstances, they have an Indefinite meaning; with Antecedents or Limiting Circumstances, they are Definite.

227. The Personal Pronoun enters into Loose Composition with the Verb of which it is the subject. In some few cases it has entered into Perfect Composition with it, as,

Buailibh—strike ye; Thogainn—I would lift; Buaileamaid—let us strike; Buaileam—let me strike. In these examples the Pronouns are in some cases old forms now in disuse.

228. EXERCISE. Translate the following sentences into English :—

Tha duine aig an dorus; tha e bochd. Thoir biadh do na h-eich; tha iad acrach. Tha guth binn aig Sìne bhig; sheinn i an t-òran gu h-anabarrach milis. Théid na gillean do 'n eilean anns a' mhaduinn; tha e fada bho thìr. Bha thu ùine fhada aig an tobar, a laochain. Falbh air tòir an fhéidh, agus till mu fheasgar. Tha e gaothar. Buailibh an dorus leis a' bhata bhuidhe. Rinn iad riombal mu 'n teine. Rachaibh do 'n eaglais. Faigh aran agus im do'n ghille bheag, tha e sgìth agus acrach. Gairm air a' chù ghlas; tha e anns an t-sabhull. Cuir ris a' mhonadh e. Thill Niall mac a' ghobhainn agus an greusaiche dubh, oir bha iad sgìth agus fann. Thug e cuireadh a dh' Iain gu banais a nighin. Fhuair mi biadh 'us deoch 'us bàigh. Théid sinn thar a' chuain. Gheibh sinn còir air tìr ar dùthchais. Togaidh sinn ar cinn gu dàna. Chì sibh an ròs fo 'n driùchd. Tha deòir air an sùilean. Togamaid càrn air a' chnoc. Eisdeam ri òraid an duin' ainmeil. Thilg Iain clach; bhuail i mo chas, agus ghèarr i i. Thuit an t-òrd air mo chois, agus bhrùth e i.

229. **Demonstrative Pronouns.**—The Demonstrative Pronouns refer to Relative Position, and save much

labour in description. They are only Approximately Definite, and are limited to a certain extent by circumstance. They are as follows:—

So = here, refers to a place nearer to the speaker, or First Person, than to the hearer, or Second Person, as,

Tha clach an so. } A stone is here.
Is stone in here.

Sin = there, refers to a place nearer to the Second Person than to the First Person, as,

Tha clach an sin. } A stone is there.
Is stone in there.

Sud (*siod*) = yonder, refers to a place so far removed that it is useless to define its position in relation to First or Second Person, as,

Tha clach an sud. } A stone is yonder.
Is stone in yonder.

230. The Demonstrative Pronouns are often used without any verb, before a noun or subject, as,

So am fear. } Here is the man.
Here the man.

231. They also stand for things in positions corresponding to the meaning of the words *so, sin, sud*, as,

Tha so blàth. } This is warm.
Is this warm.

Tha sin fuar. } That is cold.
Is that cold.

Tha sud gorm. } Yon is blue.
Is yon blue.

232. The Demonstrative Pronoun, unlike the Personal Pronoun, does not enter into Composition with the Verb of which it is the Subject. It, however, enters into Loose Composition with a Preposition preceding it, and ends a Limitation.

233. The Demonstrative Pronoun is used without a preposition, to limit a preceding noun. *Sud*, however, when so used, drops the *s* and becomes *ud*, as,

Thuit an duine so. } This man fell.
Fell the man here. }

Bhris am bata sin. } That staff broke.
Broke the staff there. }

Theich an cù ud. } Yonder dog fled.
Fled the dog yonder. }

234. The Article must always precede the Noun when *so*, *sin*, and *ud* are used after it.

235. EXERCISE. Translate the following sentences into English :—

Bha duine an so air Di-Sathuirne agus bha e liath. Sin an tobar. Gabh deoch as an tobar sin. Lìon an cupan sin le uisge fuar. Tha searrach anns an achadh ud; tha e donn. Glac an seillean sin. Tha am buachaille caoimhneil ris an treud. Sud e air a' chreig ghlais ud. Tha an sgian sin glé gheur. Ghèarr i meur a' ghiullain òig. Tha 'm bainne so blàth. Sin fear agus bean bhochd aig ceann an taighe. Bha na gillean òga anns a' bhàta so anns a' mhaduinn. Ghlac iad Pàdruig anns an àite so. Tha ribhinn òg anns a' bhaile sin. Tha sin breugach. Sud athair na ribhinn òige. Tha na ròsan llonmhor anns a' ghlaic ud. Bithibh seasmhach aig an àm so. Dèanaibh sin, fheara, agus ni sibh gu math. Tha an duine sin beairteach, ach tha am fear so bochd. Tha maigheach air an tom ud; sud i aig bun na craoibhe. Bha na fir an so, ach bha na h-eich an sud. Cuir an sin na leabhraichean. Teich as an ionad so gu luath. Cuir crioman beag càise air a' bhreacaig so. Falbh leis an duine sin. Rachamaid troimh 'n bhealach ud.

236. **Possessive Pronouns.** — Corresponding to the Personal Pronouns there are Pronouns, called Possessive Pronouns, which precede the Noun, and denote Possession or Property in the Noun, as,

Tha thu acrach; gabh do dhinneir. } You are hungry; take your
Are you hungry; take your dinner. } dinner.

237. *Do* corresponds in meaning to *thu*, but besides that, it indicates that *thu* possesses, has a right to, or property in, *dinneir*. The Possessive Pronouns are as follows :—

Mo = my,
Do = thy or your,
A (left out before Vowels) = his,
} which aspirate the Consonants following them.

A (*a h-* before Vowels) = her, which does not aspirate the Consonant following it.
Ar (*ar n-* before Vowels) = our.
Ur (*bhur*), (*ur n-* and *bhur n-* before Vowels) = your—plural.
An (*am*) = their.

238. These Pronouns enter into Composition with Nouns following, and Prepositions preceding, them. *Do* becomes *t'* before Vowels and *fh*, except when preceded by a Preposition ending in a Vowel, as *air t' each* (on your horse); but *do d' each* (to your horse); *air t' fheusaig* (on your beard); but *do d' fheusaig* (to your beard).

239. EXERCISE. Translate the following sentences into English :—

Tog do làmh, Eòghainn. Tha t' athair aig taobh an teine. Tha na daoine aig an fhaing agus tha an coin air an toman ud. Fheara, fheara, bithibh caoimhneil ris a' bhrùid bhochd sin. Tha bhur làmhan salach; nighibh iad aig an tobar. Glanaibh ur casan anns an t-sruth so. Tha ar n-eich air a' mhachair. Tha falt buidhe air an nighin òig ud, agus tha a sùilean gorm. Tha feusag an duine so ruadh, agus a shùilean donn. Chaochail maduinn ait ar n-òige. Bi saoithreach an àm do neirt agus t' òige. Tha a sùilean caomh 's a ghàire faoin. Bha maduinn m' òige subhach blàth. Dùisg, a Ghàidhlig,' s tog do ghuth. Togaidh i le buaidh a ceann. Bithibh seasmhach, mo chàirdean, aig an àm so. Dhùin i a sùil anns a' chadal bhuan. Fhuair mi gealladh daingeann, teann bho mo ribhinn òig. Thog a' bhean bhochd a làmhan. Cuir t' each anns an stàbull. Gheibh na

saighdearan buaidh air an naimhdean. Togaibh bhur làmhan.
Tha ar n-athair sean. Seinnidh mi duan do ghille mo luaidh.
Bhris an gobha 'òrd. Faigh Alasdair gu luath; thuit 'each anns a' pholl. Shrac i a h-aparan.

240. **Secondary Meanings of Prepositions.**—As stated at ¶ 168, Prepositions are applied to express relations other than those of space. A few instances of this extended application are introduced here for use in the succeeding exercises.

Air = on, expresses the relation of a creature to its own mental state, as,

Tha eagal air an duine. } The man is afraid.
Is fear on the man.

Fo = under, is used for a similar purpose, as,

Tha an duine fo eagal. } The man is afraid.
Is the man under fear.

Aig = at, expresses the idea of possession, as,

Tha leabhar aig Anna. } Ann has a book.
Is book at Ann.

Le = with, expresses the idea of absolute possession, as,

Is le Anna an leabhar. } The book belongs to Ann.
Is with Ann the book.

Ann = in, is used in the assignment of an object to a new class, the relation being conceived as existence in the new class, as,

Tha an duine 'na (ann a) shaor. } The man is a wright.
Is the man in-his wright.

Tha i 'na bantraich. } She is a widow.
Is she in-her widow.

241. **Prepositional Pronouns.**—The Prepositions and the Personal Pronouns, from much coming in contact, have entered into Perfect Composition, as,

Théid thu leam.
Théid thu le mi. } You will go with me.
Will go you with me.

242. They may end a Limitation. They are limited in number, and the following is a complete list:—

PREPOSITIONAL PRONOUNS.

	Singular			Plural		
1	2	3	3	1	2	3
me	you	him	her	us	you	them
mi	tù	è	i	sinn	sibh	iad

			Air = on.			
orm	ort	air	oirre	oirnn	oirbh	orra
			Aig (ag) = at.			
agam	agad	aige	aice	againn	agaibh	aca
			Ann = in.			
annam	annad	ann	innte	annainn	annaibh	annta
			As (à) = out of.			
asam	asad	as	aiste	asainn	asaibh	asta
			De = of, and off.			
diom*	diot	deth	dith	dinn	dibh	diù
			Do = to.			
domh*	duit	dà	di	duinn	duibh	doibh(daibh)
			Eadar = between.			
—	—	—	—	cadarainn	eadaraibh	eatorra
			Fo = under.			
fodham	fodhad	fodha	foidhpe	fodhainn	fodhaibh	fodhpa
			Gu = to.			
h-ugam	h-ugad	h-uige	h-uice	h-ngainn	h-ugaibh	h-nea
			Le = with.			
leam	leat	leis	leatha	leinn	leibh	leò (leotha)
			Mu = about.			
umam	umad	uime	uimpe	umainn	umaibh	umpa
			O (bho) = from.			
uam†	uait	uaith(e)	uaipe	uainn	uaibh	uapa
			Ri = towards.			
rium	riut	ris	rithe	ruinn	ribh	riù (riutha)
			Roimh (romh) = before.			
romham	romhad	roimhe	roimpe	romhainn	romhaibh	rompa
			Thar = over, across.			
tharam ‡	tharad	—	thairte	tharainn	tharaibh	tharta
			Troimh (tromh) = through.			
tromham	tromhad	troimhe	troimpe	tromhainn	tromhaibh	trompa

* Compounds of *de* and *do* frequently have their Initial Consonant aspirated, as, *dhlom, dhomh,* etc. (¶ 96.)

† *Uam, uait,* etc., frequently have the forms *bhuam, bhuait,* etc.

‡ These Prepositional Pronouns are not much used, the following forms being preferred, *thairis orm, thairis ort, thairis air,* etc.

THE FUNCTIONS OF WORDS. 63

243. Prepositional pronouns are also used in a Formal way, like è, as:—

Tha a casan ris. ⎫
Are her feet towards it. ⎭ Her feet are exposed, or bare.

Tha e gu math dheth. ⎫
Is he well off it. ⎭ He is well off.

Tha an dìle ann. ⎫ There is rain.
Is the rain in it. ⎭ It is raining.

244. The pronouns included in *ris, dheth*, and *ann* are the Formal è, which does not mean anything.

245. EXERCISE. Translate the following sentences into English:—

Tha leabhraichean ùra againn. Tha mulad orm. Thug mi crioman arain dà. Cuir dhìot do bhoineid. Tha sporran fada aige. Thoir dhomh do làmh, a charaid. Tha leabaidh shocair fodham. Falbh leis do 'n bhaile. Cuir umad do chleòca; tha 'n oidhche fuar. Labhair e gu caoimhneil ris. Imich thusa romham. Rach thairis air an t-sruth. Ghoid e an sgian bheag bhuaidh. Tha tàirneanach ann. Cuir dhìot do chòta fliuch, agus cuir ort an deacaid thioram so. Rachamaid trompa anus a' mhaduinn. Cuir uait an leabhar, agus innis duinn sgeul, no seinn òran. Thubhairt mi rithe, "Innis sin do Cheit." Sheall i orm gu h-iochdmhor caoin. Thoir leat mo shoraidh gu mo chàirdean anns a' ghleann. Ràinig sinn an dachaidh lom; bha gearan agus osnaich throm ann. Bha eagal mór orra. Bha i leam anns a' bhaile mhór. Thàinig sinn o Thìr nam beann, tìr a' chaoimhneis, tìr a' chàirdeis. Fhuair iad buaidh le buillean cruaidh. Cuir foidhpe do bhreacan. Chuir Seònaid oirre a boineid agus a gùn sìoda, agus chaidh i do 'n eaglais. Rachainn leibh do 'n mhonadh, ach thàinig mo mhac á Sasunn. Théid mi leibh anns a' mhaduinn. Thug iad uaibh na srathan 'us na glinn. Tha iad fo bhròn. Tha crioman arain aig a' phàisde. Tha aoibhneas air na fìr. Is le Eachann an t-each donn, ach is le Eanraig an làir bhàn. Tha Eóghann 'na dhuine gòrach. Tha Ealasaid 'na boirionnach tapaidh. Bha Alasdair 'na ghaisgeach. Tha sùrd air na gillean.

246. Some of the Prepositions enter into more or less Close Composition with the Possessive Pronouns, as follows:—

PREPOSITIONS BEFORE POSSESSIVE PRONOUNS.

	Singular.			Plural.		
1	2	3	3	1	2	3
my	your	his	her	our	your	their
mo	do	a	a (h-)	ar (ar n-)	ur (ur n-)	an

Aig (ag) = at.

| 'gam* | 'gad | 'ga | 'ga (h-) | 'gar (n-) | 'gur (n-) | 'gan† |

Ann = in.

| 'nam | 'nad | 'na | 'na (h-) | 'nar (n-) | 'nur (n-) | 'nan |

De = of, and off.

| de m' | de d' | de' | de' (h-) | de 'r (n-) | de 'r (n-) | de 'n |

Do = to.

| do m' | do d' | d' a | d'a (h-) | d' ar (n-) | d' ur (n-) | d' an |

Fo = under.

| fo m' | fo d' | fo' | fo' (h-) | fo 'r (n-) | fo 'r (n-) | fo 'n |

Gu = to.

| gu m' | gu d' | g' a | g' a (h-) | g' ar (n-) | g' ur (n-) | g' an |

Le = with.

| le m' | le d' | le' | le' (h-) | le 'r (n-) | le 'r (n-) | le 'n |

Mu = about.

| mu m' | mu d' | m' a | m' a (h-) | m' ar (n-) | m' ur (n-) | m' an |

O (bho) = from.

| o m' | o d' | o' | o' (h-) | o 'r (n-) | o 'r (n-) | o 'n |

Ri = towards.

| ri m' | ri d' | ri' | r' a (h) | ri 'r (n-) | ri r (n-) | r' an |

Roimh (romh) = before.‡

| romh m' | romh d' | romh' | romh' (h-) | romh 'r (n-) | romh 'r (n-) | romh 'n |

Troimh (tromh) = through.‡

| tromh m' | tromh d' | tromh' | tromh' (h-) | tromh 'r (n-) | tromh 'r (n-) | tromh 'n |

* This series is only used before the Verbal Noun (or Present Participle), as, 'gam thogail (literally, at my lifting)—lifting me.
† The n of the Third Person Plural becomes m before Labials.
‡ Roimh and troimh are the forms most commonly used; romh and tromh are given because of the limited space.

THE FUNCTIONS OF WORDS. 65

247. EXERCISE. Translate the following sentences into English :—

Tha an cù fo d' chathair. Cuir an neapaicinn so mu d' mhuineal. Innsidh iad sin d' ar n-aithrichean. Sgrìobh le d' laimh dheis e. Thàinig an cù sin o d' thigh. Rinn mi an gnothuch fo 'r sùilean. Bhruidhinn i r' a companach gu feargach. Fhreagair esan i gu caoimhneil. Chaidh an sionnach troimh m' ghàradh. Bruidhinn r' an companaich. Tha iad fior mìbheusach. Cuir an cleòc so in' a guailnean. Thoir am paipear sin d' a h-athair. Tha Art agus Ailean 'nad thigh. Bithibh uasal 'nur giùlan agus coisnibh onoir d' ar dùthaich. Tha iochd 'us càirdeas 'na gnùis. Tha guth na cuthaig air do stùcan. Tha e de m' chinneadh. Fhuair na giullain nathair bheag fo 'n chloich. Mharbh iad i le 'm batachan. Tog a' chlach sin agus cuir an té so 'na h-àite. Theich an gille bradach roimh m' athair. Ceilibh fo 'r n-aparan e. Thugamaid d' ar n-aithrichean e. Goididh sinn na ràimh as am bàtaichean. Faic a' chearc agus a h-àl. Ghiùlain i an leanabh g' a athair. Sgrìobh i litir g' a h-athair.

248. Unaccented Emphasising Suffixes.—These are used with the Personal, Possessive, and Prepositional Pronouns, and vary according to the Person of the Pronoun. They are always used at the end of a Limitation, as follows :—

1. SING. Mise, mo chù-sa, mo chù luath-sa, leam-sa.
   I or me, my dog, my swift dog, with me.
2. ,, Thusa (tusa), do chù-sa, do chù luath-sa, agad-sa.
   You or thou, your or thy dog, your or thy swift dog, at you.
3. ,, Esan, a chù-san, a chù luath-san, air-san.
   He or him, his dog, his swift dog, on him.
   Ise, a cù-se, a cù luath-se, aice-se.
   She or her, her dog, her swift dog, at her.
1. PLUR. Sinne, ar cù-ne, ar cù luath-ne, umainne.
   We or us, our dog, our swift dog, about us.
2. ,, Sibhse, ur cù-se, ur cù luath-se, annaibhse.
   You, your dog, your swift dog, in you.
3. ,, Iadsan, an cù-san, an cù luath-san, riù-san.
   They or them, their dog, their swift dog, towards them.

E

249. **Accented Emphasising Suffix.**—The word *féin*, or *fhéin*, is used with the Personal and Possessive Pronouns in every way like the Unaccented Emphasising Suffix. It is accented always, and is found both as *féin* and *fhéin* without any regard to rule. For example:—

Mi fhéin, mo chù fhéin, mo chù luath fhéin.
Myself, my own dog, my own swift dog.
Sibh féin, ur cù fhéin, ur cù luath fhéin.
Yourselves, your own dog, your own swift dog.
Leam féin, agad fhéin, umainn fhéin.
With myself, at yourself, about ourselves.

250. **Indefinite Pronouns.**—The Indefinite Pronouns are *có, cia, ciod*, and *cuin*. They are used formally, and stand for Unknown Terms. When placed at the beginning of a sentence they are used Interrogatively, i.e., they indicate a question: an indefinite term is put forward for solution. The Indefinite Pronouns are generally used without a verb, as,

Có è an duine sin?
Who he the man there? } Who is that man?

Ciod è an obair sin?
What it the work there? } What is that work?

Cia meud a th' agad?
How much is at-you? } How much have you?

Cia as a thàinig thu?
Where out-of came you? } Whence came you?
Where did you come from?

Cuin a dh' fhalbh thu?
When went you? } When did you go?

Innis domh có a bh' ann.
Tell to-me who was in it. } Tell me who was there.

Innis dà ciod a bh' aige.
Tell to-him what was at-him. } Tell him what he had.

Cum dhuit fhéin cia meud a th' agad.
Keep to-you self how much is at-you. } Keep to yourself how much you have.

Innis domh cuin a théid thu.
Tell to-me when will-go you. } Tell me when you go.

THE FUNCTIONS OF WORDS. 67

251. EXERCISE. Translate the following sentences into English :—

Tha thusa cèarr. Tha mise ceart. Tha mo làmh chlì-sa goirt. Tha ultach mór aige-san. Thug iadsan leò un leabhraichean do 'n sgoil. Bhris mi mo chaman fhéin agus fhuair mi am fear so bho m' charaid òg an so. Gabh h-ugad fhéin e; tha feum agad air. Innis domh có è an gille fada, caol sin. Cia as a thug thu an t-each bàn sin, a sheanair? Cuin a théid na daoine so as ar tigh-ne? Tha mi sgìth dhiù. Thug thu fhéin am buille trom dha. Bhuail a bhàta-san air an sgeir agus chaidh i fodha. Tha peann agus dubh agaibh-se, ach tha paipear geal agam-sa. Cia lion éisg a thug sibh as an amhainn? Ghlac sinne móran éisg. Ceannaichidh sinn gùn ùr d' ar mathair-ne. Có thusa, a dhuine ladarna? Ciod è do bharail-sa, fhir mo chridhe? Bhruidhinn mi fhéin ris gu math sgaiteach. Fhreagair e gu sèimh mi. Tha ar n-each donn-ne aig a' chèardaich. Thig mo phiuthar òg-sa air Di-ciadain. Falbhaidh ur bràthair-se air Di-màirt. Tha a gùn ùr-se dubh. Tha boineid ghorm aige-san. Tha gruaidhean dearga aice-se. Ghèarr mi mo chorrag-sa leis an sgian. Tha faobhar mo sgine-sa anabarrach geur.

252. **Numerals.**—Numerals are words denoting Number. They precede nouns and follow the article; and all three enter into Loose Composition.*

253. **Cardinal Numerals.**—The Cardinal Numerals denote Number, without regard to Order, e.g.—

Thuit trì clachan. }
Fell three stones. } Three stones fell.

254. *Clachan* limits *trì*, and *trì clachan* together limit *thuit*. These numerals, with the exception of 1, 2 and

---

* It has been usual to class the Gaelic Numerals with the Adjectives. There is no apparent reason for so doing. The two parts of speech have nothing in common. The Adjective limits the Noun, whereas the Noun limits the Numeral.

20 and its multiples, require to be followed by nouns in the Plural Number.

255. The Numeral Particle.—When the Numerals point back to an Antecedent, they do not require the repetition of the Noun. In answer to the question, "How many stones fell?" it suffices to state the number without a noun, thus, "Three." But when the Gaelic Numeral is so used, a meaningless particle is introduced before it, after the manner set forth in the Table of Numerals (see Index). The Particle, however, is subject to elision, e.g.—

Thuit a tri. } Three fell. { Thuit tri.
Fell three. }   { Fell three.

256. Ordinal Numerals.—Another class of Numerals, based on the Cardinal Numerals, and denoting Order, are called Ordinal Numerals, e.g.—

Thuit an treas clach. } The third stone fell.
Fell the third stone. }

257. When the Ordinal Numerals point back to an Antecedent, they do not require the repetition of the antecedent noun; but its place is given to a word having a very general application commonly, *fear* for Masculine nouns and *té* for Feminine nouns. In answer to the question, "Which of the stones fell?" the answer might be:—

Thuit an treas té.   } The third one fell.
Fell the third one.   }

Thuit an coigeamh té deug. } The fifteenth one fell.
Fell the fifth one ten.   }

258. If, instead of *clach*, the antecedent were *gille*, the answer might be:—

Thuit an treas fear deug. } The thirteenth one fell.
Fell the third one ten.   }

THE FUNCTIONS OF WORDS. 69

259. Exercise. Translate the following sentences into English :—

Tha trì dorsan air an tigh. Shrac an gille beag deich duilleagan as an leabhar. Tha ochd litrichean deug anns an aibideil. Leag a' ghaoth dà fhichead craobh anns a' choille. Leughamaid an treas caibideal deug thairis air an dà fhichead. Mharbh an cat dà luchag dheug. Sheas mi anns an àite so còig mionaidean deug ar fhichead. Tionndamaid gus a' cheathramh salm deug thairis air an t-sè fichead. Cia meud rud a tha agad an sin? Tha fichead 's a h-aon deug. Thoir dhòmhsa iad. Ghèarr Iain còig fichead slat 's a trì. Tha sin breugach. Ghèarr mi-fhéin trì fichead 's a h-ochd té deug dhiù. Bha ceithir air fhichead fear agus còig air fhichead piobaire ann. Ghlac na fir eatorra mìle, còig ceud, trì fichead 's a dhà. Innis duinn àireamh nan saighdear a tha anns a' bhuidhinn ud. Trì fichead fear 's a h-aon deug. Aireamh iad gu ceart. Tha dà fhear dheug thairis air an trì fichead ann. Thuit trì mìle, dà cheud agus còig fir dheug anns a' chath fhuilteach sin. Tha mac an t-saoir mu dhà bhliadhna dheug a dh'aois. Tha 'athair dà fhichead 's a sè.

260. Impersonal Verbs.—Statements are often made without regard to any Subject, i.e., facts are predicated without regard to cause or origin. The verbs used in such cases are called Impersonal. It is principally Transitive Verbs which are so used, but Intransitive and Substantive Verbs come in likewise for the same treatment, e.g.—

Thogadh an duine. ⎫
Lifted-was the man. ⎭ The man was lifted.

Buailear an cù. ⎫
Struck-will-be the dog. ⎭ The dog will be struck.

Thàtar ag radh. ⎫ It is said.
Are at saying. ⎭ They say.

261. It is customary to regard Nouns following such Verbs, as the Subjects of the Verbs; but that is not so. A noun following an Impersonal Verb, is its Object.

The only Subject which an Impersonal Verb can be said to have, is that indefinite one contained in the terminations *adh* and *ar*. In the older language, nouns which followed Impersonal Verbs, took the Accusative case, and not the Nominative. The Accusative case, which corresponded to what is commonly called the Objective in English Grammar, is no longer in the language.

262. EXERCISE. Translate the following sentences into English :—

Crochar am mortair. Cuirear an gaduiche am priosan. Thogadh na siùil bhàna ris a' chrann àrd. Chuireadh an tuagh air an t-samhaich cheirt. Cluinnear na h-eòin anns a' Chéitean. Bhuaileadh an dorus le slait. Thogadh a' chlach throm le fear làidir. Lìonadh am botul le fìon. Tòisichear ri tubbadh an taighe. Brisear a' chlach mhór sin an ceann deich mionaidean. Dhìonadh an dùthaich le claidheamhan móra ar sinnsir. Ghlacadh e 'na lìon fhéin. Gearrar do sgòrnan le d' theangadh fhéin. Nìtear càrn mór de chlachan beaga.

263. **Limitation by Verb.**—Hitherto the Verb was the principal part of speech in a sentence, and the other words were used singly, or in groups, to limit it. The Verb is now to be considered as a Limitation to other parts of speech. The words which verbs limit are of a Formal character, having no definite meaning of themselves, but, by their presence and position, giving significance to the groups of words in which they occur. They are called Verbal Particles. Only the most important are to be introduced at this stage. A Verb limiting a Particle expressed or understood, is said to be used Conjunctively, e.g.—

(Do) bhris mi e. } I broke it.
— broke I it. }

Am bris mi e? } Shall I break it?
— shall-brea'k I it. }

264. When the Verb is used without a Particle expressed or understood, it is said to be used Independently, as,

Brisidh mi e.
Will-break I it. } I will break it.

Brisear e.
Will-be-broken it. } It will be broken.

265. **The Verbal Particles.**—The Verbal Particles may be classed as Simple and Composite. The Simple Particles are the Article *an*, the Prepositions *gu* and *do*, which are merely Assertive, and *na*, which is Negative. The Composite Particles are made up of the Simple Particles which have entered into composition with one another, in some cases Close, and in others Perfect. They are as follows:—

Gu'n = gu an; old form, *con = co an.*
Nach, cha, cha'n = na gu an; old form, *nachon = na co an.*
Nach = an na gu an; old form, *nachon = an na co an.*

266. **The Verbal Article An.**—That *an* (*am*) is a form of the same Article which is used before Nouns, is proved by the fact that Prepositions like *le* and *ri* add an *s* when they come before it (¶ 196). Like some of the Pronouns and the Article for Nouns, its powers are determined by Circumstance, e.g.—

Am bris mi a' chlach?
—shall-break I the stone. } Shall I break the stone?

So a' chlach air am bris   mi i.
Here the stone on — will-break I it. } This is the stone on which I will break it.

So an t-òrd leis am bris   mi e.
Here the hammer with—will-break I it. } This is the hammer with which I will break it.

267. In the first example, the Article has no Antecedent. It is therefore Indefinite, and, as it were, put forward for solution. It is the Index of a Question.

In the other examples, owing to its having an Antecedent, it has the value of a Pronoun. It points back to *clach* and *òrd*, and may be translated "which" or "whom," as the nature of the Antecedent requires it.

268. **The Verbal Preposition Gu.**—The Preposition *gu* is used only before the Article. At the beginning of a sentence, i.e., when not limiting another word, it is merely Assertive, and cannot be rendered in English.* In other circumstances it can be rendered by "that," e.g.—

Gu'n gabh   iad e. ⎫
— will-take they it. ⎭ They will take it.

Innis dà   gu'n gabh   iad e. ⎫
Tell to-him — will-take they it. ⎭ Tell him (that) they will take it.

269. **The Verbal Preposition Na.**—The Preposition *na* negatives the verb before which it is placed. Only the Imperative forms of the verb—those which express a desire or command—can follow it. As already shown, *na* enters into composition with *gu'n* and produces the Composite Particles *nach*, *cha'n* and *cha*. *Nach* is the best preserved form, but lacks the final *un* or *'n*. *Cha'n* retains the final *un* before Vowels, while the initial *na* is left out. *Cha* is used before Consonants, and is the most decayed form, having dropped a particle at both ends. *Cha* and *cha'n* are used before Principal Verbs, usually found at the beginning of a sentence. *Nach* is used when the Verb with its Particle is a Limitation of another word.† *Cha* aspirates all aspirable con-

* The use of *gu'n* at the beginning of a sentence, is almost confined to narrative and poetry.

† In certain districts, *nach* is still the form of the word in some cases where *cha* is commonly used; for instance, before a Principal Verb preceded by other words, as, *A réir coltais* nach *sguir e an nochd* (According to appearance, it will not stop to-night) for *A réir coltais* cha *sguir e an nochd*.

sonants except *d* and *t*, and *b* of the word *bu.** *Cha'n* always, and *nach* sometimes, aspirate *f*, e.g.—

Na bris a' chlach.
Not break the stone. } Do not break the stone.

Cha bhris mi a' chlach.
Not will-break I the stone. } I will not break the stone.

Cha'n iarr mi deoch.
Not will-seek I drink. } I will not seek a drink.

Innis dà nach bris   mi a' chlach. } Tell him I will not break
Tell to-him not will-break I the stone. } the stone.

270. The second *nach*, given at ¶ 265, partakes of the powers of the Article, being, like it, Interrogative at the Beginning of a Sentence, and Pronominal after an Antecedent; and the Prepositions *le*, *ri*, *ann*, etc. (¶¶ 196, 266), become *leis*, *ris*, *anns*, etc., before it, e.g.—

Nach bris mi a' chlach?
Not shall-break I the stone. } Shall I not break the stone?

So a' chlach air nach bris   mi i. } This is the stone on which
Here the stone on not will-break I it. } I will not break it.

So an t-òrd leis nach bris   mi i. } This is the hammer with
Here the hammer with not will-break I it. } which I will not break it.

271. **The Verbal Preposition Do.**—All the preceding examples contain verbs in the Future Tense. By the introduction of *do*, the verbs are put in the Past Tense without the necessity of Terminal Inflection, e.g.—

Thuit clach.   An do bhris i? } A stone fell. Did it break?
Fell stone.   — — broke it. }

So a' chlach air an do bhris mi i. } This is the stone on which I
Here the stone on — — broke I it. } broke it.

---

* With many *s* is unaspirated after *cha*, as, *Cha seas mi fada* (I will not stand long).

So   an   t-òrd   leis an do bhris mi i. } This is the hammer with
Here the hammer with — — broke I it. } which I broke it.

Gu'n do ghabh iad e. } They took it.
— — took they it. }

Innis dà gu'n do bhuail iad   e. } Tell him (that) they struck it.
Tell to-him — — struck they it. }

Cha do bhris mi a' chlach. } I did not break the stone.
Not — broke I the stone. }

Cha d'iarr mi deoch. } I did not seek a drink (¶ 103).
Not — sought I drink. }

Innis dà nach do bhris mi e. } Tell him (that) I did not break it.
Tell to-him not — broke I it. }

Nach do bhris mi e? } Did I not break it?
Not — broke I it. }

So a' chlach air nach do bhris mi i. } This is the stone on which I
Here the stone on not — broke I it. } did not break it.

So   an   t-òrd   leis nach do bhris mi i. } This is the hammer with
Here the hammer with not — broke I it. } which I did not break it.

272. Although *do*, as we see, when used after a Particle, invariably introduces a Past Tense, it cannot be said to be the Index of Past Tense,* for we find it

---

* The Index of Past Tense was formerly *ro*, which was usually preceded by *do*, a preposition seemingly of the same value as *gu*. When aspiration after *ro* became an established fact, *ro* was no longer required, as the Aspiration became the Index, and *do* was left in contact with the verb. *Do* is undergoing the same process. It is being left out where its purpose is sufficiently served by Aspiration. For that reason, *do* is rarely used before a Principal Verb, which usually has its place at the beginning of a sentence. It is preserved before Vowels in the form *dh'*, where Aspiration cannot possibly supplant it. *Do* and *ro* are preserved together in the words *gu'n d'ràinig, gu'n d'ruy*, and provincially in *gu'n d'robh*. *Do* is preserved provincially before a Principal Verb when it happens to be preceded by other words, as, *A mach a (do) ghabh na fir* (Out went the men) (footnote to ¶ 269).

THE FUNCTIONS OF WORDS. 75

used for limiting nouns, in the Future as well as in the
Past, e.g.—

Tog a' chlach a (do) thuit. } Lift the stone which fell.
Lift the stone — fell.

Togaidh tu a' chlach a (do) thuiteas. } You will lift the stone
Will-lift you the stone — will-fall. } which will fall.

273. The Independent Verbs before, and the Conjunctive Verbs after *clach* in the above examples, are expressed in the Negative as follows:—

Na tog a' chlach nach do thuit. } Do not lift the stone which did
Not lift the stone not — fell. } not fall.

Cha tog thu a' chlach nach tuit. } You will not lift the stone
Not will-lift you the stone not will-fall. } which will not fall.

274. EXERCISE. Translate the following sentences into English:—

An do bhuail duine an dorus? An toir mi biadh do na h-eich? Nach téid na gillean do'n chladach? Na rach do'n bhaile mhór gus an till t'athair. Cha chuir mi an cù ris a' mhonadh. Cha'n iarr mi ni bhuaidh. Glac am fear a ghoid na dearcagan. So an giullan air an do thuit geug na craoibhe. Na innis do m' mhàthair gu'n do ghèarr mi mo chorrag leis an sgian gheur. Innsidh mi dhi nach till thu gu feasgar. Cha'n òl mi deoch làidir. Tha e fior gu'n do thill an saighdear. Thoir dhomh do sgian gus an gèarr mi am maide so. Cha'n fhàs ni air an fhearann thana sin. An croch iad an duine a ghoid an t-airgead? Cha chroch; ach cuiridh iad am priosan e. Cha d' àireamh thu an t-airgead gu ceart; tha ceithir tasdain deug agad 'nad laimh agus dà fhichead 's a tri air a' bhòrd. Dùin do shùilean agus fosgail do bheul, agus feuch ciod a ni mi. Cha dùin 's cha'n fhosgail. Mharbhadh tri eòin leis an aon urchair. So an deicheamh fear a thàinig gus an dorus eadar seachd uairean 'sa mhaduinn agus meadhon latha. Nach do chuir thu bainne 'sa chupan? So duine bochd nach d' fhuair biadh. Feòraich dheth ciod a ghabhas e. Cha tig fiaclan duit ach na fiaclan a thàinig. Cha tig fuachd gus an tig an t-Earrach. Na tog mi gus an tuit mi. Cha d' éirich an duine gus an d' fhalbh an gille. So an t-each air am marcaich mi do'n bhaile. Thàinig na h-iasgairean do'n eilean anns a' bhàta aca fhéin. Sin am bàta a reic mi fhéin riù. Nach do phàigh iad thu? Am faigh thu dhomh soitheach anns an cuir mi na dearcagan so? Tha e fìor nach fàg na daoine an gleann gus an tig an Samhradh.

275. **The Substantive Verbs.**—The Substantive Verbs merely assert, without implying action. They are *bi*, *tha* (*ta*), *bheil* (*'eil*), *is* and *bu*. Of these, only *bi* undergoes inflection.

276. **The Verb Bi.**—The Verb *bi* is used Independently and Conjunctively, and is inflected after the same principles as other verbs, with the exception of a slight irregularity in the Past Tense. The Past Tense is *bha* after *a* (*do*) when the Verb is used as a Limitation of a Noun, or as the Predicate at the Beginning of a Sentence. It is *robh* after the Article and the Composite Particles containing the article, e.g.—

Bi sàmhach. Be quiet.
Am bi thu sàmhach? \
— will-be you quiet. / Will you be quiet?
Bha mi sàmhach. \
Was I quiet. / I was quiet.
An robh thu sàmhach? \
— were you quiet. / Were you quiet?
Am fear a (do) bha sàmhach. \
The man — was quiet. / The man who was quiet.
Nach bi thu sàmhach? \
Not will-be you quiet. / Will you not be quiet?
Cha bhi mi sàmhach. \
Not will-be I quiet. / I will not be quiet.
Nach robh thu sàmhach? \
Not were you quiet. / Were you not quiet?
Am fear nach robh sàmhach. \
The man not was quiet. / The man who was not quiet.

277. **The Verb Tha.**—*Tha*, or *ta*, is used to express Present Tense, and takes before it one particle only, namely *a*, which has the same power as *a* (= *do*), e.g.—

Tha mi fuar. } I am cold.
Am I cold. }

Am fear a tha fuar. } The man who is cold.
The man— is cold. }

278. **The Verb Bheil.**—*Bheil* is used after the Article and Composite Particles expressed or understood, with the same meaning as *tha*. In entering into composition with the Particles it suffers a change of form,* e.g.—

Am bheil thu fuar? } Are you cold?
— are you cold. }

Gu'm bheil thu fuar. } You are cold.
— are you cold. }

Cha 'n 'eil thu fuar. } You are not cold.
Not are you cold. }

Nach 'eil thu fuar. } Are you not cold?
Not are you cold. }

279. **The Verb Is.**—*Is* is used for the same purpose as *tha* when the Predicate is to be Emphasised. When *is* is used, the Predicate may not be divided (¶ 169). *Is* is used Independently, and Conjunctively with *a* (*do*) only after Nouns and Pronouns. It is not used in conjunction with the Article and Composite Particles at all. These are used without any verb expressed, with the same power as if *is* were present. What should naturally be *gu'n* takes the form *gur*. But *gu'n* is nevertheless found in some localities, though rarely

---

* Assuming *feil* to have been the old form of this verb, these changes are explainable thus: *Bheil* is due to the Eclipsis of *f* after *m* of the Article *am*; *'eil* is due to the Aspiration of *f* after *cha* and *nach* as formerly noticed at ¶ 269, *'eil* being equivalent to *fheil*.

in literature. Consideration of *is* as a Limitation to Nouns and Pronouns is reserved for a future stage.

Is duine treun Seumas. }
Is man brave James. } James is a brave man.

Is fuar an t-uisge. }
Is cold the water. } The water is cold.

Am fuar an t-uisge? }
— cold the water. } Is the water cold?

Gur fuar an t-uisge. }
— cold the water. } The water is cold.

Cha'n fhuar an t-uisge. }
Not cold the water. } The water is not cold.

Nach fuar an t-uisge? }
Not cold the water. } Is not the water cold?

280. **The Verb Bu.**—*Bu* is used with the powers of *s*, but for the expression of Past Tense, e.g.—

Bu duine treun Seumas. }
Was man brave James. } James was a brave man.

B' fhuar an t-uisge. }
Was cold the water. } The water was cold.

Am b' fhuar an t-uisge? }
— was cold the water. } Was the water cold?

Gu'm b' fhuar an t-uisge. }
— was cold the water. } The water was cold.

Cha b' fhuar an t-uisge. }
Not was cold the water. } The water was not cold.

Nach b' fhuar an t-uisge? }
Not was cold the water. } Was not the water cold?

281. EXERCISE. Translate the following sentences into English:—

Am bheil each Ruaraidh bàn? Tha; agus tha làir Sheumais donn. Is binn an ceòl a tha anns an tigh mhór. Nach bu dearg an teine? Thubhairt Ealasaid gu'm bu bhlàth an là air an d' thàinig i do'n ghleann. Nach fuar an t-sìd a tha ann. Cha robh na fir fada anns a' mhonadh. Is gille foghainteach an coigreach òg. Cha'n 'eil Alasdair aig an eaglais. Cha'n òrdugh bata aig bàillidh. Cha'n 'eil m' earball fo 'chois. Cha'n 'eil i beag bòidheach, no mòr grànda. Is l àigheil duine r' a dhream. Is blàth anail na màthar. Na bi cùramach uime. Nach mise a bha gòrach! Am bheil na coin agad, a Thormaid? Gur e mo cheisd an t-òigear. Gur trom, trom mo cheum o'n là a chaill mi do spéis. Is geal an sneachd air mullach na beinne. Nach 'eil an leanabh math? Nach robh na dearcagan milis? An robh thu tinn, a Cheit? Shiubhail an duine bochd a bha euslan. Cha bhi mi umhail duit-sa. Buailidh mi an ceud fhear nach bi beusach. Na bi 'nad amadan. Tha Sine 'na màthair do'n leanabh òg. Am fior gu'm bheil Peigi ceithir bliadhna deug a dh' aois? Is truagh nach 'eil mi 'nam dhuine beairteach. Agus nach 'eil thu beairteach? Is tu a tha beairteach. Tha neart, slàinte agus òige agad. Nach math gu'n d' thàinig an t-uisge? Cha'n e sin mo bheachd air.

282. **The Verbal Noun.**—The Verbal Noun is formed from the primitive form of the verb by adding a suffix. That most commonly found is *adh* or *eadh*, as *glan* (clean), *glanadh* (cleaning). Other suffixes serving the same purpose are *ail, eil; inn, ainn; achd, eachd;* etc. Some Verbal Nouns are without Terminal Inflection, as *òl* (drink), *òl* (drinking). The Verbal Noun ending in *adh* is inflected for the Genitive case only. All are indeclinable in the other cases and have no Plural. A noun limiting a Verbal Noun is in the Genitive case.

283. The principal use to which Verbal Nouns are put, is to express Continuous or Progressive Action, after the preposition *a'*, or *ag*, preceded by the Substantive Verbs *bi* (in all its cases), *tha* and *bheil*, e.g.—

Tha iad a' bualadh chlachan. } They are striking stones.
Are they at striking of-stones. }

Bithidh iad 'gam bualadh le òrd. } They will be striking
Will-be they at their striking with hammer. } them with a hammer.

Am bheil iad ag éisdeachd? } Are they listening?
Are they at listening. }

284. The Verbal Adjective.—The Verbal Adjective is formed from the primitive form of the verb by adding the suffix *te* (*ta* and *da*), as *buail* (strike), *buailte* (struck); *fosgail* (open), *fosgailte* (opened).* The Verbal Adjective is indeclinable, but suffers Aspiration after the manner of ordinary adjectives.

285. The Verbal Adjective is used with the Substantive Verbs *bi, tha, bheil, is* and *bu,* to express what is called in the grammar of other languages the Passive Voice, e.g.—

Tha an dorus fosgailte. } The door is open.
Is the door opened.

Bithidh an dorus fosgailte. } The door will be open.
Will-be the door opened.

Am bheil an dorus fosgailte? } Is the door open?
— is the door opened.

Is fosgailte an dorus. } The door is open.
Is opened the door.

Bu dùinte an dorus. } The door was shut.
Was shut the door.

286. Exercise. Translate the following sentences into English :—

Tha an t-each bàn a' ruith gu math luath. Tha an tuathanach òg pòiste. Tha Seumas beag a' sracadh nan duilleagan as an leabhar. Tha an duine a' leughadh a' Bhìobuill. Cuin a bha an tigh togte? Tha an obair mhath a rinn mi millte. Eisd ris an luinneig bhinn a tha Mórag a' seinn. Tha an cù a' tabhann-

---

* In adding the suffix *te*, the rule that consonants must come between vowels of the same class is not in every case regarded, because in speech it is not conformed to. In the case of Verbs of one syllable ending in *l, n, r,* or *s,* and all those of more than one syllable, an *i* is introduced before the final consonant to make the spelling accord with the pronunciation. For the same reason it is left out in other cases.

aich. Tha an cléireach a' sgrìobhabh litreach d'a mhaighstir. Am bheil daoine a' dol, no a' pilltinn? Na bi a' gearradh a' bhùird le do sgian. Tha na fir ag òl drama 'san tigh-òsda. Thàtar ag innseadh gu'm bheil Eachann a' dol do thir chéin. An innis thu so dhomh? Am bheil càirdean agad an Sasunn? Cha'n 'eil; ach tha bràthair agam an Eirinn. Bha Tómas ag innseadh dhomh gu'n robh am balla leagte. Có a leag e? Am bheil an t-ùrlar sguabte? Tha mo chridhe briste, brùite. Tha an ceò ag iathadh mu na stùcan àrda. Nach bòidheach am bàta a' seòladh air an fhairge le a siùil bhàna sgaoilte ris a' ghaoith? Cha tuit caorau á cliabh falamh. Tha na fir a' lomairt nan caorach. Am bheil mòran diù rùisgte? Bha an duine a' labhairt gu h-ealanta ris an t-sluagh. Tha am feur a' fàs gu math. Tha a' chuid mhór de 'n arbhar buainte.

287. **Accent in Composition.**—The sense of a sentence often depends on the way in which the voice is modulated. But that fact cannot be very well illustrated through the medium of written language. Some of the essential principles may however be taught.

288. As a rule words which Complete a Limitation receive the Accent, as shown by the following examples in which the accented words are given in italic letters:—

Thuit *clach*. Thuit clach *bheag*.

289. In the second example, *clach* being unaccented, indicates to the mind that the conception of *clach* is to be suspended until more is heard. *Bheag* follows then, to limit the application of *clach*, and, getting the accent, indicates that the limitation is complete. A sentence ending on an unaccented word (pronouns excepted) is very disappointing, because it gives rise to the idea that something is withheld.

290. In the following sentence there are two accented words, each ending a limitation:—

Thuit clach *bheag* air an *làr*.

291. Pronouns may end a limitation without receiving the accent. They are on that account said to enter into Composition with the Verb. In general, it is Loose Composition, but in one or two cases (¶ 227) it is Perfect:—

    Togaidh mi e.   Togar iad.   Tog a' chlach so.

292. The pronouns *mi, e, iad* and *so* are unaccented. If Emphasis is wanted, the Emphatic Suffix is added to the Personal Pronouns, and then they get the Accent. The Demonstrative Pronoun is emphasised by Accent only, as,

    Togaidh mis' e.   Togar iadsan.   Tog a' chlach so.
    I will lift it.   *They* will be lifted.   Lift *this* stone.

293. The Prepositional Pronouns end Limitations, and receive the Accent. The Prepositional Pronouns, *leis, ris, as, air* and *ann* are always Accented, whereas the Prepositions of the same spelling, never ending a limitation, are Unaccented, e.g.—

    Cuir *boineid* air a' cheann.   Cuir *boineid air*.
    Put a bonnet on his head.   Put a bonnet on him.

294. EXERCISE. Write out sentences from the preceding exercises, and draw a line underneath the Accented Words.

SECTION V.

WORDS IN REGARD TO THE CHANGES THEY UNDERGO IN FULFILLING THEIR FUNCTIONS IN THE EXPRESSION OF THOUGHT.

295. **Inflections of the Verb.**—The Verb is inflected by adding suffixes to the Primitive form, which is that used to give a command. These inflections express one Tense only, namely, the Future. Past Tense is expressed without inflection (¶ 154). Only a few Verbs have Present Tense (¶¶ 276, 7, 8, 9.)

296. **Tense.**—The Future Tense is expressed in two ways: 1. The Direct Future, referring to the time forward from the instant of speaking; 2. The Indirect Future, for which a present is assumed, either in the future or the past, for the purpose of looking forward from that.

297. **Voice.**—There are two Voices: 1. The Personal Voice, which is that used when a subject is expressed (¶ 149); 2. The Impersonal Voice, which is that used when no subject is expressed (¶ 260).

298. **Mode.**—The Verb is used in two Modes: 1. The Independent Mode, which requires no Particles to bring out its meaning, or relation to the context; 2. The Conjunctive Mode, which requires the Verb to have Particles before it, of which it is a Limitation (¶ 263).

These Particles are not always expressed. Forms of the Verb in the one Mode must not be confounded with similar ones in the other. Though alike, they have different values.

299. Mood.—The Independent Verb has two Moods representing the relation of the Speaker to his own expressions: 1. The Imperative Mood, which conveys a desire expressed as a command; 2. The Assertive, which conveys an expression of opinion.*

300.

PARADIGM OF THE INDEPENDENT VERB.

FUTURE TENSE.

IMPERATIVE MOOD.

Direct.

Personal.

1. Glac = Catch.

Indirect.

2. Personal.	3. Impersonal.
Glacadh = Let — catch.	Glac(t)ar† = Let — be caught.

ASSERTIVE MOOD.

4.	Direct.	5.
Glacaidh‡ = Will catch.		Glacar = Will be caught.

6. Verbal Adjective.	7. Verbal Noun.
Glacte§ = Caught.	Glacadh = Catching.

---

* All such moods as Negative, Interrogative, Optative, etc., are expressed, not by the Verb, but by the Particles.

† The *t* of the Imp. Impersl. is frequently left out; but its retention is recommended in all cases.

‡ In certain parts of the North Highlands the Fut. Ass. Dir. Persl. is *Glacas*, as, *Glacas mi e* (I will catch him).

§ See footnote to ¶ 284.

301. The Imp. Dir. Persl. takes the Pronoun into Perfect Composition when the Second Person is Plural, as,

  Glacaibh = Catch ye. Glacaibhse—Emphatic.

302. In the Secd. Pers. Sing., the Pronoun is not spoken except when emphasis is required; and then it is *thusa* which is used, as,

  Glac so = Catch this. Glac thusa so = Catch you this.

303. The Imp. Indir. Persl. takes the First Personal Pronouns into Perfect Composition, as,

  Glacam = Let me catch. Glacamaid = Let us catch.
  Glacam-sa—Emphatic. Glacamaide—Emphatic.

304. The suffix *maid* is a pronoun now obsolete except in this connection.

305. **The Verbal Preposition Na.**—The Imp. forms of the Ind. Verb are used Conjunctively with *na* (¶ 269), as follows:—

  Na glac iad = Do not catch them.
  Na glacadh e an ròpa = Let him not catch the rope.
  Na glactar an ròpa = Let not the rope be caught.

306. Exercise. Translate the following sentences into English:—

Gabh do dhiunneir. Gabhadh iad an t-airgead. Leumam air a' charraig. Tuitidh na craobhan móra. Na buailtear na gillean beaga. Bruidhinnear riu. Loisgear am fraoch. Togamaid iolach àrd. Na teicheadh na coigrich. Fàsaidh an gille mór. Na bogtar 'san allt iad. Tiormaichear air an fheur iad. Brisear an geataichean. Na leagtar an tighean. Gearrar na ròpan fada. Leughtar an leabhar leò-san a tha foghluimte. Na pòsadh iad. Dùisgear am pàisde. Sgrìobhaidh mi litir. Sgrìobhadh iad an ainmean air an leacan. Na dùineadh Eachann an dorus.

Dannsadh na caileagan. Leumaibh anns a' bhàta. Sguireamaid de 'r n-amaideachd. Togam a' chlach mhór so. Cuidichibh Màiri. Innsear an naigheachd daibh-san. Rachamaide gus a' chladach. Glanam-sa m' aodach. Na buailibhse an cat. Tha an giullan a' sracadh an leabhair. Tha mo bhata briste.

307. EXERCISE. Translate the following sentences into Gaelic :—*

Strike the door. Do not lift a stone. Let him break the stone. Let us take our food. Listen to (ri) the birds. Let the men lift their hands. The child will awaken. The boy will cut his finger. The tale will be told to us. The boy's finger will be cut. They will write a letter. Fill you the bottle with milk. The chair will be broken. Let not the door be opened. The man is lifting his hands. His hand was lifted to (ri) his head. The shepherd is leaving the glen. The place is deserted. The boy is reading a book. Knock down the wall. Listen to the sound of the trumpet. The window is broken. Do not tell that tale. Let not that man be struck. She is breaking sticks with an axe.

308. The Verbal Preposition Do.—Certain forms of the Verb are used after *do* with varying effect, as follows :—

PARADIGM OF THE VERB CONJOINED TO *DO.*

ASSERTIVE MOOD.

PAST TENSE.

8. Personal.	9. Impersonal.
(a=do) Ghlac=Caught.	(a=do) Ghlacadh=Was caught.
(a) Dh' fhill=Folded (¶ 123).	(a) Dh' fhilleadh=Was folded.
(a) Dh' Iarr=Sought.	(a) Dh' iarradh=Was sought.

* After careful explanation by the teacher. As for the simpler exercises in the translation of English into Gaelic, they can be set by the teacher himself from the matter afforded by the Gaelic-English Exercises.

THE INFLECTIONS OF WORDS. 87

FUTURE TENSE.
Direct.

10. Personal.
(a) Ghlacas = Will catch.
(a) Dh' fhilleas = Will fold.
(a) Dh' iarras = Will seek.

11. Impersonal.
(a) Ghlacar = Will be caught.
(a) Dh' fhillear = Will be folded.
(a) Dh' iarrar = Will be sought.

12. Indirect. 13.
(a) Ghlacadh = Would catch.
(a) Dh'fhilleadh = Would fold.
(a) Dh'iarradh = Would seek.

(a) Ghlactcadh* = Would be caught.
(a) Dh'fhillteadh = Would be folded.
(a) Dh'iarrteadh = Would be sought.

309. The Past Impersl. must not be confounded with the Fut. Indir. Persl. of the same form. The latter has an expressed Subject; the former is followed by an Object and has no expressed Subject (¶ 260).

310. The Fut. Indir. Persl. takes the Pronoun in the First Persons Sing. and Plur. into Perfect Composition, as,

Ghlacainn = I would catch. Ghlacamaid = We would catch (¶ 227).

311. The Particle is, as a rule (¶ 92 and footnote ¶ 272), elided at the beginning of a sentence or before a Verb which is not a Limitation. When the Verb is a Limitation the Particle is retained usually in the form *a* or *a dh'* (¶ 123).

312. The Fut. Dir. is only used as a Limitation of a Subject or Object, except in the North (footnote ¶ 300).

313. The following examples illustrate the verb as a Principal Verb and as a Limitation :—

Ghlac iad fear. They caught a man.
Am fear a ghlac iad. The man (whom) they caught.
Ghlacadh fear leò. A man was caught by them.
Am fear a ghlacadh leò. The man who was caught by them.

* See footnote to *Glacte* (¶ 284), which applies with equal force in this case.

88   GAELIC GRAMMAR.

Am fear a ghlacas iad (¶ 272).* { The man (whom) they will catch.
                                  The man who will catch them.
Am fear a ghlacar leò.   The man who will be caught by them.
(do) Ghlacadh iad fear. They would catch a man.
Am fear a ghlacadh iad (¶272). { The man (whom) they would catch.
                                  The man who would catch them.
(do) Ghlacteadh fear leò. A man would be caught by them.
Am fear a ghlacteadh leò. The man who would be caught by
                             them.

314. **The Verbal Article An.**—Certain forms of the verb are used after *an* and the Composite Particles into whose composition it enters (¶ 265) as follows:—

PARADIGM OF THE VERB CONJOINED TO *AN*, ETC.

ASSERTIVE MOOD.

FUTURE TENSE.

Direct.

14. Personal.	15. Impersonal.
Glac = Will catch.	Glacar = Will be caught.

16.   Indirect.   17.
Glacadh = Would catch.   Glacteadh = Would be caught.

PAST TENSE.

18.   Direct.   19.
Do ghlac = Caught.   Do ghlacadh = Was caught.
D'fhill = Folded.   D'fhilleadh = Was folded.
D'iarr = Sought.   D'iarradh = Was sought.

315. The Fut. Indir. Persl. takes the Pronoun into Perfect Composition, as formerly shown at ¶ 310.

* The context, or other circumstances, must regulate whether the Noun or Pronoun after the Verb is the Subject or Object. It is in cases such as this, the loss of the Accusative Case is felt. This example of the Conjunctive Fut. is negatived by *nach* on the same principle as the Independent Fut. is negatived by *cha* (¶ 273), as.

Cha   tog   mi a' chlach nach tuit. } I will not lift the stone which
Not will-lift I the stone not will-fall. }   will not fall.

THE INFLECTIONS OF WORDS. 89

316. The powers of the Verb in its Conjunctive forms after *an* and the Composite Particles, are very fully illustrated in the following examples:—

An (am).—Interrogative without an Antecedent, Pronominal with one (¶ 267).
An glac mi e? Will I catch him?
An là air an glac mi e. The day on which I will catch him.
An glacar e? Will he be caught?
An là air an glacar e. The day on which he will be caught.
An glacadh iad e? Would they catch him?
An là air an glacadh iad e. The day on which they would catch him.
An glacteadh e? Would he be caught?
An là air an glacteadh e. The day on which he would be caught.
An do ghlac iad e? Did they catch him?
An là air an do ghlac iad e. The day on which they caught him.
An do ghlacadh e? Was he caught?
An là air an do ghlacadh e. The day on which he was caught.
Gu'n (gu'm). *Gu* makes the preceding list Affirmative (¶ 268).
Gu'n glac mi e. I will catch him.
Tha iad ag ràdh gu'n glac iad e. They say (that) they will catch him.
Gu'n glacar e. He will be caught.
Tha iad ag ràdh gu'n glacar e. They say (that) he will be caught.
Gu'n glacadh iad e. They would catch him.
Tha iad ag ràdh gu'n glacadh iad e. They say (that) they would catch him.
Gu'n glacteadh e. He would be caught.
Tha iad ag ràdh gu'n glacteadh e. They say (that) he would be caught.
Gu'n do ghlac iad e. They caught him.
Tha iad ag ràdh gu'n do ghlac iad e. They say (that) they caught him.
Gu'n do ghlacadh e. He was caught.

Tha iad ag ràdh gu'n do ghlacadh e. They say (that) he was caught.

Cha, cha'n, nach. *Na*, which is in the composition of these particles, negatives the immediately preceding list. *Nach* is the form which is used when the verb is a Limitation. *Cha* and *cha'n*—the former before Consonants, and the latter before Vowels—are the forms used when the Verb is not a Limitation (¶ 269).

Cha ghlac mi e. I will not catch him.
Cha'n òl mi e. I will not drink it.
Tha iad ag ràdh nach glac mi e. They say (that) I will not catch him.
Am fear nach glac { The man (whom) they will not catch.
iad (¶ 313†). { The man who will not catch them.
Cha ghlacar e. He will not be caught.
Tha iad ag ràdh nach glacar e. They say (that) he will not be caught.
Am fear nach glacar leò. The man who will not be caught by them.
Cha ghlacadh iad e. They would not catch him.
Tha iad ag ràdh nach glacadh iad e. They say they would not catch him.
Am fear nach glacadh { The man (whom) they would not catch.
iad (¶ 313†). { The man who would not catch them.
Cha ghlacteadh e. He would not be caught.
Tha iad ag ràdh nach glacteadh e. They say (that) he would not be caught.
Cha do ghlac iad e. They did not catch him.
Tha iad ag ràdh nach do ghlac iad e. They say (that) they did not catch him.
Am fear nach do ghlac { The man (whom) they did not catch.
iad (¶ 313†). { The man who did not catch them.
Cha do ghlacadh e. He was not caught.
Tha iad ag ràdh nach do ghlacadh e. They say (that) he was not caught.
Am fear nach do ghlacadh leò. The man who was not caught by them.

Nach. *An*, which enters into the composition of this particle at its beginning, adds the power of the Article to the immediately

THE INFLECTIONS OF WORDS. 91

preceding list, making the Composite Particle Interrogative without an Antecedent, and Pronominal with one (¶ 270). This *nach* must not be confounded with the *nach* of the preceding list. The former never—except provincially in a few places, and then to a restricted extent—goes before a Verb which is not a Limitation of a noun or another verb. The latter *nach* is used before Principal Verbs to ask a question in the Negative, and is used as a Limitation only to Prepositions expressed or understood.

Nach glac mi e? Will I not catch him?
An t-àite anns nach glac mi e. The place in which I will not catch him.
Nach glacar e? Will he not be caught?
An t-àite anns nach glacar e. The place in which he will not be caught.
Nach glacadh iad e? Would they not catch him?
An t-àite anns nach glacadh iad e. The place in which they would not catch him.
Nach glacteadh e? Would he not be caught?
An t-àite anns nach glacteadh e. The place in which he would not be caught.
Nach do ghlac iad e? Did they not catch him?
An t-àite anns nach do ghlac iad e. The place in which they did not catch him.
Nach do ghlacadh e? Was he not caught?
An t-àite anns nach do ghlacadh e. The place in which he was not caught.

317. EXERCISE. Translate the following sentences into English :—

Ghlac na gillean dóbhran donn. C' àite an do ghlacadh e? Dh' ith Uilleam bonnach mór. Cuin a dh' ith e e? A' cheud té a sheinneas òran, gheibh i duais. An rud a dh' iarrar air, cha diùlt e. Ghabhainn deoch-bhainne. Bhuaileadh air an t-sròin e. Bhuailteadh e le fear làidir. Am fear a ghoideas, cuirear am priosan e. An tog thu do làmh chli? Am buailear an t-iarunn. An éisdeadh iad riut? Gu'n d' éirich mi 'sa mhaduinn. Fhuair mi fios gu'n do chaochail e. Thàtar ag innseadh gu'n do phòs e. Cha bhruidhinn mi ris. Am buaileadh tu an giullan nach do thog làmh riut? Cha sheinneadh iad òran no laoidh. So an t-àite anns an iarramaid na dearcagan. Sud an t-àite anns an togadh a' chlann tighean beaga. Nach fan thu sàmhach? So an geata a leagadh leis an each bhàn. Bha rìgh Eirionn toilichte leis an fhreagradh a fhuair e. Cha bhruidhneadh iad ris a' chloinn òig. Tha mi a' smaointeachadh gu'n do theich an coigreach. Nach itheadh e aran? Dh' iarradh air bualadh, agus bhuail e. Tha sinn gu math aithnichte anns an àite so. Ghearradh an sgian sin im, tha mi a' creidsinn. Faiceam an tu fhéin a th' ann. Fhreagradh ise iad am briathran mìne. Nach innseadh tu dhaibh do chor? Am fear nach treabh air muir, cha treabh e air tìr. Am fear nach teich, teichear roimhe. Am fear nach fosgail a sporran, fosglaidh e a bheul. Am fear nach cunntadh rium, cha chuntainn ris. Am fear a phòsas bean, pòsaidh e dragh. Cha d' òl an sagart ach an deoch a bh' aige. Cha mheallar am fear glic an dara uair. Cha dèan aon smeòrach samhradh. Cha chreid an òige gu'n tig aois, 's cha chreid an aois gu'n tig bàs. Na cuir do spàin an càl nach buin duit. Rùisgeadh e a thigh fhéin agus thubhadh e tigh a choimhearsnaich. Thàinig fios gu'n do bhàthadh iad. Bha iad a' bagairt gu'm marbhadh iad an cù.

318. EXERCISE. Translate the following sentences into Gaelic (¶ 307 *):—

They took food. They sought a drink. She spoke to (ri) me. The man who listened to the tale. The tree was struck by the axe. The door which will be opened. The window which she would open. The hare which would be caught. The house which they built. Will you drink at the well? Did you lift the stone? Will the wall be knocked down? The time at which we will take our dinner. The day on which we mended the boat. The year in which the house was burned. They told (to) the man that his cow was stolen. News came that the boy was drowned. I will not ask his book. I did not steal the key. It is not true that he broke his leg. It is likely that he will not write to his father. It is likely the wall would be knocked down. The horse would not run. The boy would not yield. They said that the school was built by him. Will you not row, Magnus? Were you not oppressed by it? The fishes which were caught. The meat which was prepared. The place in

which they hid him. The stone under which it would be put.
The book on which he spent the shilling. The hammer with
which he will strike the anvil. The girl spoiled her frock. My
heart is broken. They are not afraid (under fear) that I will
deceive them. He is sure that Mary will speak to him. The
house that Alexander bought is not falling. The bird will not
sing. The boat would not move.

319. **Inflection of Nouns.**—The naming or setting
forth of the various modes in which nouns are inflected,
is called Declension. Various ways have been adopted
for this; but the following will perhaps be found as
practical as any.

320. In trying to find out the particular way in
which a noun is declined, the following questions have
to be considered in their order :—

1. Is the final vowel Low (Broad) or High (Small)?
2. Is the noun of one, or of more than one, syllable?
3. Is the noun Masculine or Feminine?
4. Does any fact exclude it from the Principal type of declension?
5. Does any fact relegate it to a Subordinate type?

321. **The Gender of Nouns.**—The Gender of Nouns is
determined as follows :—

MASCULINE NOUNS.

322. GENERAL RULE.—Nouns whose Final Vowels are Low
(Broad) are mostly of the Masculine Gender, particularly if they
are of more than one syllable, subject always to the undernoted
Particular Rules—some of which are contradictory to the General
Rule—and to the fact that many nouns require their gender to
be learned by Experience.

323. PARTICULAR RULES.—1. Names of Male Objects, as,
fear, man ; *tarbh*, bull.

2. Names of the Young of Animals regardless of sex, as, *uan*,
lamb ; *laogh*, calf ; *isean*, gosling.

3. **Names of Trees**, as *darach*, oak ; *giubhas*, fir.

94   GAELIC GRAMMAR.

4. Derivatives in *an* denoting Diminutiveness, as, *crioman*, little bit; *gogan*, little dish.
5. Derivatives in *as*, as, *càirdeas*, friendship; *sonas*, happiness.
6. Derivatives in *adh*, as, *aoradh*, worship. The Verbal Noun in *adh* is Masculine.
7. Derivatives in *air, eir, ir, ear, ach* and *iche*, mostly denoting agent or doer, as, *sealgair*, hunter; *taillear*, tailor; *fleasgach*, young man ; *piobaire*, piper ; *maraiche*, sailor.

FEMININE NOUNS.

324. GENERAL RULE.—Nouns whose Final Vowel is High (Small) are mostly Feminine, subject to the undernoted Particular Rules, certain exceptions to be found in the preceding list, and other individual exceptions which have to be learned by Experience.

325. PARTICULAR RULES.—1. Names of Female Objects, as, *bean*, woman ; *màthair*, mother.

2. Names of Countries, as, *Albainn*, Scotland ; *Eirinn*, Ireland ; *An Eadailt*, Italy. *Sasunn*, England, is Masculine.
3. Nouns denoting Species, as, *gabhar*, goat ; *caora*, sheep (with considerable exceptions).
4. Names of Musical Instruments, as, *clàrsach*, harp ; *druma*, drum ; *tromb*, jew's-harp.
5. Names of Trees collectively, as, *giubhasach*, fir plantation; *droighneach*, clump of hawthorn bushes.
6. Names of the Heavenly Bodies, as, *grian*, sun ; *gealach*, moon.
7. Names of Diseases, as, *a' bhreac*, the smallpox ; *a' bhuidheach*, the jaundice.
8. Derivatives in *ag*, denoting Diminutiveness, as, *cromag*, crook ; *abhag*, terrier ; *caileag*, girl.
9. Derivatives in *achd*, as, *lànachd*, fulness ; *rioghachd*, kingdom.
10. Derivatives in *e*, denoting an Attribute, as, *buidhre*, deafness ; *leisge*, laziness.
11. Derivatives in *ad*, denoting an Attribute, as, *gilead*, whiteness ; *lughad*, smallness.
12. Monosyllables in *ua* (with considerable exceptions), as, *tuagh*, axe ; *bruach*, bank.

THE INFLECTIONS OF WORDS. 95

326. A few nouns have their Gender unsettled, and some few are Grammatically of one Gender, while the objects of which they are the name, are of the opposite Sex. In regard to the latter the Adjective agrees with the Noun in Gender, while the Pronoun agrees with the Sex.

327. Nouns are divided into Two Declensions regulated by the Final Vowel. The First Declension includes all nouns whose Final Vowel is Low (Broad). The Second Declension includes all nouns whose Final Vowel is High (Small).

328. PARADIGMS OF THE FIRST DECLENSION.

NOUNS OF ONE SYLLABLE.

Masc.   (a)   Fem.
Without the Article.

	Sing.	Plur.	Sing.	Plur.
N.	clàr.	clàir.	bròg.	brògan.
G.	clàir.	chlàr.	bròige.	bhròg(an).
D.	clàr.	clàir.	bròig.	brògan.

With the Article (¶ 193) and Voc. Part. (¶ 179).

	Sing.	Plur.	Sing.	Plur.
N.	clàr.	clàir.	bhròg.	brògan.
G.	chlàir.	clàr.	bròige.	bròg(an).
D.	chlàr.	clàir.	bhròig.	brògan.
V.	chlàir.	chlàra.	bhròg.	bhrògan.

329. It must be understood that any Unaspirated Case is subject to Aspiration after words which cause Aspiration (¶ 93), as, Nom. *mo chlàr;* Gen. *mo bhròige.* It is the Final Inflection which determines case, except in the Gen. Plur. without the Article, which is always Aspirated. Keeping these facts in view, it will be unnecessary in the sequel to give Paradigms with the Article.

330. It is usual in grammars to give the Dat. Plur. in *ibh;* but that is so very uncommon in modern written and spoken practice—the Scriptures excepted—that it may be classed among Obsolete Inflections.

331. Masculine Nouns introduce *i* before the Final Consonant to form the Gen. and Voc. Sing., and the Nom. and Dat. Plur. The Voc. Plur. adds *a* to the Nom. Sing. The Gen. Plur. without the Art. is formed by Aspirating the Nom. Sing.

332. Feminine Nouns introduce *i* before the Final Consonant in the Gen. and Dat. Sing., at the same time adding *e* to the Gen. They form the Plur. by adding *an* in all the cases, which is frequently elided in the Gen. The Voc. is formed by Aspirating the Nom. both in the Sing. and Plur. respectively.

333. **Change of Vowel.**—Some nouns in forming their cases suffer a Change of Vowel wherever *i* is introduced, as follows:—

334. *O* changes to *u*, as in *toll, tuill; tonn, tuinn; gob, guib; sop, suip; tom, tuim; sloc, sluic; torc, tuirc; crodh, cruidh; long, luing,* etc. So also *clay (cloy), cluig; càrn, cùirn.*

335. *A* before *ll* and *nn* changes to *o*, as, *dall, doill; clann, cloinn,* etc. So also *clach (cloch), cloich; cas (cos), coise;* etc.

336. *Eò* changes to *iù* before *l,* as, *ceòl, ciùil; seòl, siùil.*

337. *Eu* changes to *eò* before *l, n* and *r,* as, *beul, beòil; eun, eòin; feur, feòir;* etc. So also *leus, leòis; gleus, gleòis.* But *geug, géig; breug, bréig;* etc.

338. *Ia* changes to *é,* as, *iasg, éisg; iall, éill; fiadh, féidh; grian, gréin; Dia, Dé;* etc. But *sgian,* Gen. *sgéine* or *sgine; biadh,* Gen. *bìdh.*

339. *Ea* gives place to *i,* as *leac, lic; cearc, circ; fear, fir; preas, pris; ceann, cinn;* etc. But *each, eich; feary, feirg;* etc.

340. *Io* gives place to *i,* as, *slol, sìl; lion, lìn;* etc.

THE INFLECTIONS OF WORDS. 97

341. Nouns of More than One Syllable.

	Masc.		(b)		Fem.
	Sing.	Plur.	Sing.	Plur.
N.	bodach.	bodaich.	gruagach.	gruagaichean.
G.	bodaich.	bhodach.	gruagaich(e).	ghruagach (aichean).
D.	bodach.	bodaich.	gruagaich.	gruagaichean.
V.	bhodaich.	bhodacha.	ghruagach.	ghruagaichean.

342. Nouns of this class follow in the main those of Class (a), the additions to the Gen. Sing. and Plur. Fem. being of rare occurrence.

343. Nouns whose Final Vowels are *ea* change the *a* into *i*, as, *faileas, faileis*, etc.

344. Many Masculine Nouns ending in *l*, *n*, or *r*, add *an* for the Plur., as, *tàillear, tàillearan; buideal, buidealan; cuilean, cuileanan*, etc.

345. Some Nouns, mostly ending in *l* or *r*, add *ichean* to form the Plur., as, *tobar, tobraichean; ceangal, ceanglaichean*, etc. These are subject to Syncope (¶ 141).

346. Most Nouns in *nn*, in forming the Plur. add *an* and Syncopate both in the Plur. and Gen. Sing., as, Nom. *buidheann*, Gen. *buidhne*, Plur. *buidhnean*, etc.

347. Nouns of One or More Syllables.

	(c)		Masc. and Fem.	(d)
	Sing.	Plur.	Sing.	Plur.
N.	loch.	lochan.	beum.	beumannan.
G.	loch(a).	loch(an).	beum(a).	bheum(annan).
D.	loch.	lochan.	beum.	beumannan.
V.	loch.	locha(*n* in Fem.)	bheum.	bheumanna(*n* in Fem.)

	(e)			(f)	
N.	gàd.	gàdaichean.		còta.	còtaichean.
G.	gàd(a).	ghàd(aichean).		còta.	chòta(ichean).
D.	gàd.	gàdaichean.		còta.	còtaichean.
V.	ghàd.	ghàdaiche(*an* in Fem.)		chòta.	chòtaiche(*an* in Fem.)

G

348. The Nouns of the preceding four classes are practically Indeclinable in the Sing., and, with the exception of the Voc., have practically also the same forms throughout the Plur., as the Gen. has usually the added syllables.

349. Some Nouns coming under (*e*) and (*f*) take *achan* in preference to *ichean*. Some Nouns add *aichean, achan* or *annan*.

350. Nouns ending in a Vowel, as a rule follow class (*c*); but in their case, a Consonant originally belonging to the noun, is restored in the Gen. and Plur. cases, as, *cnò*, Gen. *cno(tha)*, Plur. *cnothan*, etc.; or a Consonant which may not be Radical, is inserted, as, *Dia, Dé, diathan*.

351. Some Nouns coming under class (*c*), introduce *i* in the Plur., as, *bùth*, Gen. *bùth(a)*, Plur. *bùithean* or *bùthan; là, latha, làithean*, etc.

352. PARADIGMS OF THE SECOND DECLENSION.

NOUNS OF ONE SYLLABLE.

(*a*)

	Masc.	Without the Article.		Fem.
	Sing.	Plur.	Sing.	Plur.
N.	mir.	mirean.	poit.	poitean.
G.	mir(e).	mhir(ean).	poite.	phoit(ean).
D.	mir.	mircan.	poit.	poitean.

With the Article (¶ 193) and Voc. Part. (¶ 179).

N.	mir.	mirean.	phoit.	poitean.
G.	mhir.	mir(ean).	poite.	poit(ean).
D.	mhir.	mirean.	phoit.	poitean.
V.	mhir.	mhire.	phoit.	phoitean.

353. Only a very few Nouns of One Syllable whose Final Vowel is High (Small), are Masculine. In their case, the *e* of the Gen. is frequently elided; and the Voc. Plur. differs from that of Feminine Nouns, in adding *e* only. The *e* and *ean* of the Gen. of Feminine

Nouns are also sometimes elided. There is a strong tendency to make the Gen. Plur. in the absence of the Article, dependent wholly on the Initial Aspiration. When the Article is present, it is sufficiently indicative of the case; and hence also the tendency towards Elision of the Inflection in the Gen. after the Article.

354. (b) Masc.   (c) Fem.

N. druim.	dromannan.	cuid.	codaichean.
G. droma.	dhromannan.	codach.	chodaichean.
D. druim.	dromannan.	cuid.	codaichean.
V. dhruim.	dhromannan.	chuid.	chodaichean.

355. Nouns of these two classes introduce a Low (Broad) Vowel in forming the Gen. Sing. and add two syllables in forming the Plur. cases. Most of them suffer a Change of Vowel, as, *muir, mara; greim, grama,* etc.

356. Nouns ending in a High (Small) Vowel in the Nom. restore a Lost Consonant, or insert a Consonant which may not be Radical, in the Plur., as, *nì, nithean.*

357.   Nouns of more than One Syllable.

Masc. (d)   Fem.

	Sing.	Plur.	Sing.	Plur.
N.	dorsair.	dorsairean.	ribhinn.	ribhinnean.
G.	dorsair.	dhorsair(ean).	ribhinn(e).	ribhinn(ean).
D.	dorsair.	dorsairean.	ribhinn.	ribhinnean.
V.	dhorsair.	dhorsaire.	ribhinn.	ribhinnean.

(e) Fem.   (f) Fem.

N. dùthaich.	dùthchannan.	cathair.	cathraichean.
G. dùthcha.	dhùthchannan.	cathrach.	chathraichean.
D. dùthaich.	dùthchannan.	cathair.	cathraichean.
V. dhùthaich.	dhùthchanna.	chathair.	chathraichean.

(g) Masc.   (h) Masc.

N. athair.	aithrichean.	Pige.	Pigeachan.
G. athar.	aithrichean.	Pige.	Phigeachan.
D. athair.	aithrichean.	Pige.	Pigeachan.
V. athair.	aithriche.	Phige.	Phigeachan.

358. Many Nouns of more than One Syllable, particularly those which have final *l*, *n* or *r*, are syncopated when one or more syllables are added as inflections, as, *lasair, lasraichean; amhainn, aimhne, aimhnichean; gobhainn, goibhnean; obair, oibre*, etc. But some of these, instead of being Syncopated in the Gen. in colloquial speech, suffer elision of the *e*, as, *obair*, Gen. *obair* for *obaire = oibre*.

359. A few Nouns of Two Syllables, in forming the Gen. like class (*e*) by the addition of a Low (Broad) Vowel, suffer a Change of Vowel, as, *cliamhuinn, cleamhna*.

360. The distinguishing feature of class (*g*) is the formation of the Gen. by dropping the High (Small) Vowel. The Nouns which come under this class besides *athair*, are *màthair*, Plur. *mathraichean; bràthair*, Plur. *bràithrean; seanair*, Plur. *seanairean; seanmhair*, Plur. *seanmhairean;* and *nàmhaid*, Gen. *nàmhad*, Plur. *naimhdean. Piuthar* belongs to the First Decl., being *peathar* in the Gen. and *peathraichean* in the Plur.

361. **Introduction of t in the Plural.**—Some Nouns ending in *l, le, n* or *ne*, and also the word *sliabh*, introduce a *t* in the Plur. in both Decls., as, *cùil, cùiltean; coille, coilltean; smaoin, smaointean; teine, teintean; rùn, rùintean*, and *rùntan; reul, reultan; gùn, gùintean; sliabh, sléibhtean*.

·362. It must be borne in mind that a large proportion of Nouns, particularly those of more than One Syllable, are more or less irregular; but most of them approach in the manner of their declension, some one or other of the foregoing Paradigms. It is also not infrequently the case that Nouns which are Masculine in one locality are Feminine in another.

THE INFLECTIONS OF WORDS. 101

363. EXERCISE. Translate the following sentences into Gaelic (¶ 307*):—

The poems are good. The poems of the bards are long. The clouds are dark. The point of the shoe-lace is broken. The girl's song was sweet. The sails of the ship are white. Are not the days warm? When will the pots be empty? The banks of the river are flat. The prow of the boat is towards the land. At those times men were savage. The taste of the butter is not good. The grass is growing on the top of the house. My brother's books are large and heavy. The keys are hanging on a nail. Lift the lids of the chests. Your grandfather's house is thatched with heather. A drop of blood fell on my clothes. The glens are beautiful in summer. Give him food, drink and clothes. Do not give him a drink of water. The boat is at the side of the loch. The point of the knife is sharp. The hen's leg is broken. The colour of the grass is bright. That is the blind man's staff. Put this on the top of the stone. Listen to the sound of the bell. There are three bells. The men are at work at the end of the house. The stone is at the bottom of the hole. The old man's beard is grey and the hair of his head is long. I hear the music of the mavis. I hear the mavis singing on the tree. It is a very sweet song. The tailor's needle is broken. He is sewing a coat. Yonder is a dog and three whelps. The water of the wells is dirty. Four companies of (de) soldiers came to this town. Those three towns were burned. Where (what place) did you get those five beans? Their blows were heavy. The boat is at the bottom of the loch. Their coats are grey and our bonnets are blue. Give him sixteen blows with a rod. Is it this rod? It is not. A branch of a tree fell on the boy. Open the window. Go out of the way. They had six loads on their six backs. Our portions were small. The people of that country are big. They would break the leg of the chair. Our mother is old. We met on the middle of the bridge. We came to the end of our work. The floods were great. Go with me to the top of the ben. The man's friends went away. Give it a blow with the flail. The serpent's head is small. The fishermen's nets are on the shore. They brought a fish to our house. The scales of the fish are glittering. Their noses are long and sharp.

Listen to the hum of the bee. Turn the leaves of the book. Read this chapter. We heard the neighing of horses and the sound of trumpets. Who cut your finger? Put on you your bonnet. Cut this tree with an axe. The branches were cut by the wright. They would fling you into the loch. The dog will go to the sheepfold. The price of the horse was very big. Her father's brother is sick. The music of the pipe is pleasant to the ear of the Gael. The bird's feathers are beautiful. The men are seeking a hammer. The sailors are hoisting the sails. Sing a song or tell a story. Would you cut this tree?

364. **Inflections of the Adjective.**—In trying to arrive at the proper inflections of an Adjective the following are the main points to be considered:—

1. Is the final vowel of the Adjective Low (Broad) or High (Small)?
2. Is the Adjective of one syllable, or of more than one?
3. Is the Noun to which it is attached Masculine or Feminine?

365. Adjectives may, like nouns, be divided into two Declensions. Those whose last vowel is Low (Broad) belong to the First Decl. and closely follow in the Sing. the changes which nouns of Decl. 1 (*a*) undergo. Those whose last vowel is High (Small) belong to the Second Decl. and closely follow in the Sing. the changes which nouns of Decl. 2 (*a*) undergo. In the Plur. all the cases are alike, *a* being added to nouns of one syllable for the First Decl. and *e* for the Second Decl. The greatest difficulty connected with the Adjective, is to know when to aspirate the Initial Consonant. The case inflections of the Adjective depend on the Gender of the Noun. Aspiration depends on the Inflectional Changes of the Noun, the presence of the Article and, in some cases, on the Final Consonant of the Noun and Initial Consonant of the Adjective together.

THE INFLECTIONS OF WORDS. 103

PARADIGMS OF ADJECTIVES OF FIRST DECLENSION.

ADJECTIVES OF ONE SYLLABLE.

	With Masc. Nouns of Decl. 1 (a).		Without the Art.	With Fem. Nouns of Decl. 1 (a).	
	Sing.	Plur.		Sing.	Plur.
N.	mór.	mhóra.		mhór.	móra.
G.	mhóir.	móra.		móire.	móra.
D.	mór.	mhóra.		mhóir.	móra.

With the Art. (¶ 193) and Voc. Part. (¶ 179).

N.	mór.	mhóra.	mhór.	móra.
G.	mhóir.	móra.	móire.	móra.
D.	mhór.	mhóra.	mhóir.	móra.
V.	mhóir.	móra.	mhór.	móra.

ADJECTIVES OF MORE THAN ONE SYLLABLE.
Without the Art.

	Sing.	Plur.	Sing.	Plur.
N.	biorach.	bhiorach.	chrùbach.	crùbach.
G.	bhioraich.	biorach.	crùbaich(e).	crùbach.
D.	biorach.	bhiorach.	chrùbaich.	crùbach.
V.	bhioraich.	biorach.	chrùbach.	crùbach.

PARADIGMS OF ADJECTIVES OF SECOND DECLENSION.

ADJECTIVES OF ONE SYLLABLE.

	With Masc. Nouns of Decl. 1 (a).		Without the Art.	With Fem. Nouns of Decl. 1 (a).	
	Sing.	Plur.		Sing.	Plur.
N.	binn.	bhinne.		mhin.	mine.
G.	bhinn.	binne.		mine.	mine.
D.	binn.	bhinne.		mhin.	mine.
V.	bhinn.	binne.		mhin.	mine.

ADJECTIVES OF MORE THAN ONE SYLLABLE.

	Sing.	Plur.	Sing.	Plur.
N.	fearail.	fhearail.	shoilleir.	soilleir.
G.	fhearail.	fearail.	soilleir(e).	soilleir.
D.	fearail.	fhearail.	shoilleir.	soilleir.
V.	fhearail.	fearail.	shoilleir.	soilleir.

366. In the preceding examples, the maximum of aspiration is given. The Nom. and Dat. Plur. Masc. are Aspirated only when the noun introduces an *i* as the case inflection, as, *fir mhóra*, but *lochan móra*.

367. Adjectives whose Initial Consonant is *d* or *t*, after nouns ending in *n* (and sometimes *l*, *r* and *s*), are often Unaspirated where aspiration usually takes place, as, *ceann dubh*, Gen. *cinn duibh*, Plur. *cinn dubha*.

368. The *e* of the Gen. Sing. Fem. and the *a* of the Plur. are subject to Elision. When the *e* of the Gen. Sing. Fem. is elided, there is a tendency to Aspirate the Initial Consonant of the Adjective, as, *athair na caileig bhig* for *athair na caileige bige*.

369. Many adjectives of more than one syllable are subject to Syncope in the Gen. Sing. Fem. and the Plur. cases—cases which add a syllable when the Adjective is a monosyllable—and have the *e* or *a* added always, as, *muc reamhar*, Gen. *muice reamhra* (but *eich reamhair*), Plur. *mucan reamhra* (and *eich reamhra*).

370. **Change of Vowel.**—Some adjectives suffer a Change of Vowel when *i* is introduced. The changes follow those which Nouns undergo and need not be here specified (¶ 333).

371. Adjectives ending in a Vowel, as, *beò;* a Silent Consonant, as, *fialaidh;* *chl*, as, *bochd;* *rr*, as, *cèarr;* with exceptions to be learned by experience, are indeclinable.

372. EXERCISE. Translate the following sentences into Gaelic (¶ 307*):—

The bards sang long poems. Dark clouds were in the sky. He has a large shoe. They praised the girl's sweet song. They spread the white sails to the wind. The warm days came, and the cold winter went away. The mist is on the top of the high mountain. A white shirt was on his black back. That is fresh

THE INFLECTIONS OF WORDS. 105

butter. Did you taste the new cheese? The beautiful glens are deserts. The young man cut the long grass. Give (to) me that sharp knife. The point of the sharp knife cut me. The man's grey beard is long. The farmer's brown mare is in the field. Let us go to the large town. The dirty water of the deep well is bad. Three white men fell in the hard fight. That is a heavy load. The lad's grey breeches were torn and his bonnet was dirty. Give him a heavy blow. The lame boy's foot is sore. My good lad, tell (to) me your name. Run, my little girl, and tell your mother that you are hungry. The load is on the young horse. His head is on the cold hard stone. Look on the beautiful blue sea. Give milk to the young calves. The end of the heavy stone was on the ground. The honest woman's riches were not great. They were filling the large bag. The farmer was skinning the brown bull. The masons were carving the hard stones. The farmer's son is selling the grey horse and the brown mare. Sit on the dry floor. The children sat on the green knoll, and their fathers were in the field at the end of the thick wood. A light was shining through the window of the little house in the dell. The foolish young maidens wept. He struck the boy with a long thin rod. He lifted a large armful. There are splendid churches in the large town. We came on a wet day. We went away on a dark night. Cut this branch with your sharp axe. The sick man is moving. These are fat sheep. Tell that to your faithful friend. This bird has beautiful feathers. The bold heroes fought with long sharp swords. You are speaking foolish words. There are great matters under the waves of the sea. There are two black spots on the haddock and a long tail on the whiting. He came to the end of his long tale.

TABLE OF NUMERALS.

I. CARDINAL.

(a) Without a Noun.

1 a h-aon.
2 a dhà.
3 a trì.
4 a ceithir.
5 a cóig (cùig).
6 a sè (sia).
7 a seachd.
8 a h-ochd.
9 a naoi.
10 a deich.
11 a h-aon deug (diag).
12 a dhà dheug.
13 a trì deug, etc.
20 (a) fichead.
21 a h-aon ar (air, thar) fh.
    fichead 's a h-aon.
22 a dhà ar fh.
    fichead 's a dhà.

23 a trì ar fh. etc.
    fichead 's a trì, etc.
31 a h-aon deug ar fh. etc.
    f. 's a h-aon deug, etc.
40 dà fhichead.
41 dà fh. 's a h-aon.
42 dà fh. 's a dhà, etc.
60 trì fichead, etc.
80 ceithir fichead, etc.
100 cóig f. or ceud (ciad).
112 cóig f. 's a dhà dheug.
120 sè f. etc.
200 dà cheud.
241 dà cheud dà fh. 's a h-aon.
365 trì cheud trì f. 's a cóig.
400 ceithir cheud.
500 coig ceud, etc.
1000 mìle, or deich ceud.

(b) With a Noun.

1 aon chat (masc.)
    aon bhròg (fem.)
2 dà chat.
    dà bhròig.
3 trì cait.
    trì bròdan, etc.
11 aon chat deug.
    aon bhròg dheug.
12 dà chat dheug.
    dà bhròig dheug.
13 trì cait dheug.
    trì bròdan deug, etc.

20 fichead cat.
    fichead bròg.
21 f. cat 's a h-aon.
    f. bròg 's a h-aon.
    aon chat ar (air, thar) fh.
    cat ar fh.
22 f. cat 's a dhà.
    f. bròg 's a dhà.
    dà chat ar fh.
    dà bhròig ar fh.
    dà chat fh.
    da bhròig fh.

TABLE OF NUMERALS.

23 f. cat 's a trì.
tri cait ar fh.
tri brògan ar fh.
tri cait fh.
trì brògan f.
35 f. cat 's a còig deug.
còig cait dheug ar fh.
40 dà fh. cat.
41 dà fh. cat 's a h-aon.
aon 'us dà fh. cat.
50 dà fh. bròg 's a deich.
deich 'us dà fh. bròg.
leth-cheud cat.
60 trì f. cat.
100 còig f. cat.
ceud cat.
ceud bròg.

109 còig f. cat 's a naoi.
ceud bròg 's a naoi.
naoi brògan ar a' cheud.
naoi cait ar a còig f.
120 sè f.ʃcat.
200 dà cheud cat.
da cheud bròg.
365 trì cheud cat, trì f. 's a còig.
trì cheud, tri f. 's a còig cait.
trì f. cat 's a còig ar a' cheud.
1000 mìle cat.
mìle bròg
deich ceud cat.
deich ceud bròg.

NOTES.

A on aspirates all aspirable consonants in the noun following it except *d, t,* and *s.*
Da aspirates all aspirable consonants and takes a noun in the Dative case after it, as *dà chloich.* But an adjective following a noun preceded by *dà* appears in the Nominative case aspirated, as, *dà chloich bheag, dà dhuine mhór.* If the noun is governed by a Preposition, the Adjective is in the Dative case, as, *air dà chloich bhig ; le dà dhuine mhór.*
Deug is aspirated after Feminine nouns Singular—except those ending in *d, t, s, l, n,* and *r*—and nouns forming the Plural by the introduction of *i* (like Adjectives ¶ 366).
Fichead, ceud, and *mìle* are followed by a noun in the Nom. Sing.
Ar, air, and *thar* are all used for the same purpose. *Ar* is the preferable word. They are followed by aspirated consonants.

II. ORDINAL.

1st. An t-aona cat.
an aona bhròg.
an ceud (ciad) chat.
a' cheud bhròg.
2d. an dara (dàrna) cat.
an dara bròg.
3d. an treas cat.
an trìtheamh cat.
4th. an ceathramh cat.
5th. an còigeamh bròg.
6th. an sèathamh (siathamh) bròg.

7th. an seachdamh cat.
8th. an t-ochdamh cat.
an t-ochdamh bròg.
9th. an naodhamh (naoidheamh) bròg.
10th. an deicheamh cat.
11th. an t-aona cat deug.
an aona bhròg dheug.
12th. an dara cat deug.
an dara bròg dheug.
13th. an treas cat deug.
an treas bròg dheug.

108 GAELIC GRAMMAR.

14th.	an ceathramh cat deug.
	an treas bròg dheug.
20th.	am ficheadamh cat.
	an fhicheadamh bròg.
21st.	am ficheadamh cat 's a h-aon.
	an t-aona cat ar fh.
	an t-aona cat f.
	an ŏeud chat ar fh.
	an ceud chat f.
	a' cheud bhròg fh.
22d.	an fh. bròg 's a dhà.
	an dara bròg ar fh.
	an dara bròg f.
23d.	am f. cat 's a trì.
	an treas bròg ar fh.
	an treas cat f.
35th.	am f. cat 's a còig deug.
	an còigeamh bròg dheug ar fh.
40th.	an dà fh. cat.
	an dà fh. bròg.
49th.	an dà fh. cat 's a naoi.
	an naodhamh cat ar an dà fh.
50th.	an dà fh. cat 's a deich.
	an deicheamh cat ar an dà fh.
	an leth-cheudamh cat.
60th.	an trì f. cat.
	an trì f. bròg.
80th.	an ceithir f. cat.
100th.	an còig f. cat.
	an ceudamh (ciadamh) cat.
	an ceudamh bròg.
112th.	an còig f. cat 's a dhà dheug.
	an dara cat deug ar a' cheud.
	an dara cat deug ar a' chóig f.
120th.	an sè f. cat.
128th.	an sè f. cat 's a h-ochd.
	an t-ochdamh cat ar an t-sè f.
140th.	an seachd f. cat.
160th.	an t-ochd f. cat.
180th.	an naoi f. cat.
200th.	an dà cheudamh cat.
	an dà cheudamh bròg.
247th.	an dà cheudamh cat, dà fh. 's a seachd.
	an seachdamh cat 's a dhà fh. ar an dà cheud.
1000th.	am mìleamh cat.
	am mìleamh bròg.

NOTES.

The Article is *an t-* before *aona* preceding a Masc. noun. It is *an* before *aona* preceding a Fem. noun. It is *an t-* before *ochdamh* preceding Masc. and Fem. nouns. It is *an* before *ceud* preceding a Masc. noun. It is *a'* before *cheud* preceding a Fem. noun. It is *am* before *ficheadamh* preceding a Masc. noun. It is *an* before *fhicheadamh* preceding a Fem. noun. It is *an* before *ceudamh*, and *am* before *mìleamh* preceding Masc. and Fem. nouns.

Aspiration takes place in a Fem. noun after *aona*; in Masc. and Fem. nouns after *ceud*: in the numeral *ficheadamh* preceding Fem. nouns; and in all words following *dà*.

Thairis air (¶ 242) is frequently used for *ar* (*air, thar*), as, *an dara salm deug thairis air an dà fhichead*—the fifty-second psalm.

VOCABULARY.

GAELIC-ENGLISH.

ABBREVIATIONS.

a. adjective
d. dative.
df. dative feminine.
dm. dative masculine.
fut. future.
g. genitive.
gf. genitive feminine.
gm. genitive masculine.
n. noun.
nf. noun feminine.
nm. noun masculine.
No. north.

nom. nominative.
pl. plural.
pnf. proper noun feminine.
pnm. proper noun masculine.
sg. singular.
sv. substantive verb.
unatt. pref. unattached prefix.
v. verb.
va. verbal adjective.
vn. verbal noun.
vi. verb impersonal.
voc. vocative.

NOTE.—The genitive plural of most nouns is the same as the nominative singular subject to aspiration.

A.

abhag, nf. terrier.
achadh, nm. field.
acrach, a. hungry.
aibideil, nf. alphabet.
Ailean, pnm. Allan.
aimhne, g. of amhainn.
Aindreas, pnm. Andrew.
ainm, nm. name.
ainmean, pl. of ainm.
ainmeil, a. celebrated.
àird, g. and df. of àrd.
àireamh, nf. and v. number.
airgead, nm. silver.
ait, a. joyful.
àite, nm. place.
aithnich, v. know.
aithnichte, va. known.
aithrichean, pl. of athair.

àl, nm. brood.
Alasdair, pnm. Alexander.
allt, nm. brook.
àm, nm. time.
amadan, nm. fool.
amaideachd, nf. foolishness.
America, pnf.
amhainn (or abhainn), nf. river.
anabarrach, a. exceeding.
anail, nf. breath.
Anna, pnf. Ann.
aodach, nm. clothes.
aoibhneas, nm. gladness, joy.
aois, nf. age.
aotrom, a. light.
aparan, nm. apron.
arain, g. of aran.
aran, nm. bread.

arbhar, nm. corn.
àrd, a. high.
àrda, pl. of àrd.
Art, pnm. Arthur.

bagair, v. threaten.
bagairt, vn. threatening.
bàigh, nf. kindness.
bàigheil, a. kind.
baile, nm. town.
bàillidh, nm. bailliff.
bàin, g. of bàn.
bainne, nm. milk.
balach, nm. lad, fellow.
balla, nm. wall.
bàn, a. white, fair, pale.
bàna, pl. of bàn.
banais, nf. wedding.
barail, nf. opinion.
bàrr, nm. point.
bàs, nm. death.
bàsaich, v. die.
bata, nm. staff.
batachan, pl. of bata.
bàta, nm. and nf. boat.
bàtaichean, pl. of bàta.
bàth, v. drown.
beachd, nm. opinion.
beag, a. small, little.
beaga, pl. of beag.
beairteach, a. rich.
bealach, nm. pass, gap.
bean, nf. woman, wife.
beann, g. pl. of beinn.
beinn, nf. mountain, ben.
beinne, g. of beinn.
beul (No bial), nm. mouth.
beum, nm. stroke, blow.
beusach, a. well behaved.
bha, sv. was, were, etc.
bheil, sv. is, are.
bhuaileadh, v. was struck.
bi, sv. be.
biadh, nm. food.
big, gm. of beag.
binn, a. melodious, sweet.
Biobull, nm. Bible.
biodag, nf. dirk.

astar, nm. distance.
athar, g. of athair.
athair, nm. father.

B.

biorach, a. sharp.
bithidh, fut. of bi.
blasad, nm. taste.
blàth, a. warm.
bliadhna, nf. year.
bó, nf. cow.
bochd, a. poor.
bochda, pl. of bochd.
bodach, nm. an old man.
bodhar, a. deaf.
bog, a. soft.
bog, v. dip.
boglach, nf. bog.
bòidheach, a. pretty.
boincid, nf. bonnet.
boirionnach, nm. female.
bonnach, nm. bannock.
borb, a. fierce, savage.
bòrd, nm. table.
botul, nm. bottle.
bradach, a. thievish.
bràigh, nm. upper part.
bràthair, nm. brother.
breacag, nf. scone.
breacaig, d. of breacag.
breacan, nm. plaid.
breagha (No briagha), a. splendid.
brèid, nm. napkin, towel.
breugach (No briagach), a. lying, false.
briathar, nm. word, assertion.
briathran, pl. of briathar.
bris, v. break.
brisear, vi. will be broken.
briste, va. broken.
bròg, nf. shoe.
brògan, pl. of bròg.
bròn, nm. grief.
brùid, nm. brute.
bruidhinn, v. speak.
bruidhinn, vn. speaking.
bruidhinnear, v. will be spoken.

VOCABULARY. 111

brùite, va. bruised.
brùth, v. bruise.
bruthach, nm. acclivity, brae.
bu, sv. was.
buachaille, nm. herdsman.
buaidh, nf. victory.
buail, v. strike.
buailidh, v. will strike.
bualadh, vn. striking.
buainte, va. reaped.

cadal, nm. sleep.
caibideal, pm. chapter.
caidil, v. sleep.
caidlidh, fut. of caidil.
caileag, nf. girl.
caileagan, pl. of caileag.
Cailean, pnm. Colin.
caill, v. lose.
cailleach, nf. old woman.
càirdean, pl. of caraid.
càirdeas, nm. friendship.
càirdeis, g. of càirdeas.
Cairistlona, pnf. Christina.
cairt, nf. cart.
càise, nm. cheese.
caisteal, nm. castle.
càl, nm. kail.
Calum, pnm. Malcolm.
caman, nm. shinty.
caochail, v. change, die.
caoimhneas, nm. kindness.
caoimhneil, a. kind.
caoimhneis, g. of caoimhneas.
caoin, v. weep.
caoin, a. pleasant, kind.
caol, a. thin, small.
caomh, a. gentle.
caora, nf. sheep.
caorach, g. pl. of caora.
caoran, nm. bit of peat.
caraid, nm. friend.
càrn, nm. cairn, heap.
carraig, nf. rock.
cas (cos), nf. foot.
casan (cosan), pl. of cas.
cat, nm. cat.
cath, nm. fight, battle.

buan, a. lasting.
buidhe, a. yellow.
buidheann, nf. company.
buidhinn, d. of buidheann.
buille, nm. and nf. blow.
buillean, pl. of buille.
buin, v. belong.
bùird, g. of bòrd.
bun. nm. bottom, root.

C.

cathair, nf. chair.
ceangail, v. tie.
ceann, nm. head, end; an ceann, at the end.
ceannaich, v. buy.
cearc, nf. hen.
cèardach, nf. smithy.
cèardaich, g. of cèardach.
cèarr, a. wrong.
ceart, a. right.
ceil, v. conceal.
ceilidh, fut. of ceil.
ceisd, nf. darling.
céin, a. distant.
ceirt, gm. and df. of cèart.
Ceit, pnf. Kate.
Céitean, pnm. May.
ceò, nm. mist.
ceòl, nm. music.
ceòlmhor, a. musical.
ceum, nm. step.
chaidh, v. went.
chi, v. will see.
chuala, v. heard.
chuireadh, v. was put.
chunnaic, v. saw.
chunntadh, v. would account.
cinn, v. grow.
cinn, g. sg. and nom. pl. of ceann.
cinneadh, nm. race, clan.
ciobair, nm. shepherd.
clach, nf. stone.
clachan, pl. of clach.
cladach, nm. shore.
cladh, nm. graveyard.
clag, nm. bell.
claidheamh, nm. sword.

clann, nf. children.
clàr, nm. lid, board.
cléireach, nm. clerk.
cléirich, pl. of cléireach.
cleòc(a), nm. cloak.
clì, a. left (hand).
cliabh, nm. creel.
clisg, v. startle.
cliù, nm. fame, praise.
cloich, d. of clach.
cloinn, d. of clann.
cluinnear, vi. will be heard.
cluais, d. of cluas.
cluas, nf. ear.
cnoc, nm. knoll.
coigreach, nm. stranger.
coigrich, pl. of coigreach.
coileach, nm. cock.
coille, nf. wood, forest.
coimhearsnach, nm. neighbour.
coin, nom. pl. of cù.
Coinneach, pnm. Kenneth.
Coinnich, g. of Coinneach, 166.
coinnich, v. meet.
còir, nf. right, justice.
còir, a. honest.
coirce, nm. oats.
coire, nm. corrie, dell.
cois, d. of cas.
coisich, v. walk, travel.
coisinn, v. win, gain.
coisnibh, v. win ye.
colgarra, a. ferocious.
Colla, pnm. Coll.
comhairle, nf. counsel, advice.
companach, nm. companion.
companaich, pl. of companach.
cor, nm. condition, state.
còrr, nf. heron.
corrag, nf. finger.

corruich, nf. anger.
còta, nm. coat.
crann, nm. mast.
craobh, nf. tree.
craobhan, pl. of craobh.
craoibh, d. of craobh.
craoibhe, g. of craobh.
creag, nf. rock.
creagan, pl. of creag.
creid, v. believe.
creidsinn, vn. believing.
creig, d. of creag.
crìch, d. of crìoch.
cridhe, nm. heart.
crìoch, nf. end, limit.
crioman, nm. bit.
croch, v. hang.
crochar, vi. will be hung.
crosda, a. cross, angry.
cruadal, nm. hardship.
cruaidh, a. hard.
crùbach, a. lame.
cù, nm. dog.
cuan, nm. ocean.
cuain, g. of cuan.
cuid, nf. share, portion.
cuidich, v. help, assist.
cuilean, nm. whelp, pup.
cuinneag, nf. water-stoup, pitcher.
cuinneig, d. of cuinneag.
cuir, v. put.
cuirear, vi. will be put.
cuiridh, fut. of cuir.
cuireadh, nm. invitation.
cunntadh, v. would account.
cupan (copan), nm. cup.
cùramach, a. careful.
cuthag, nf. cuckoo.
cuthaig(e), g. of cuthag.

D.

dachaidh, nf. home.
daingeann, a. firm.
dàna, a. bold.
danns, v. dance.
daoine, pl. of duine.
darach, nm. oak.
daraich, g. of darach.

deacaid, nf. jacket.
dèan (No dian), v. do.
dearcag, nf. berry.
dearcagan, pl. of dearcag.
dearg, a. red.
dearga, pl. of dearg.
deas, a. ready.

VOCABULARY. 113

dcasaich, v. prepare.
deireadh, nm. stern, hinderpart.
deis. df. of deas.
deoch, nf. drink.
deòir, pl. of deur.
Deòrsa, pnm. George.
deur, nm. tear.
dhìonadh, v. was defended.
dian, a. keen, strong.
Diar-daoin, pnm. Thursday.
Di-ceudain (No. Di-ciadain), pnm. Wednesday.
Di-luain, pnm. Monday.
dìle, nf. heavy rain.
Di-màirt, pnm. Tuesday.
dinneir, nf. dinner.
dìon, v. defend.
dìrich, v. climb, ascend.
Di-sathuirne, pnm. Saturday.
diùlt, v. refuse.
dòbhran, nm. otter.
dol, vn. going.
Dòmhnull, pnm. Donald.
donn, a. brown.
Donnachadh, pnm. Duncan.
dorch(a), a. dark.
dorsair, nm. doorkeeper.
dorsan, pl. of dorus.

dorus, nm. door.
dosach, a. bushy.
dragh, nm. trouble, bother.
draghail, a. bothersome, troublesome.
dram, nm. dram (drink of spirits.)
drama, g. of dram.
dream, nm. people.
dreathann, nm. wren.
dreathainn, g. of dreathann.
drochaid, nf. bridge.
driùchd, nm. dew.
druim, nm. back.
duais, nf. reward, prize.
duan, nm. song.
dubh, a. black.
dubh, nm. ink.
Dùghall, pnm. Dugald.
duilich, a. difficult.
duilleag, nf. leaf.
dùin, v. shut, close.
duine, nm. man.
duinn, g. of donn.
dùisg, v. awaken.
dùthaich, nf. country.
dùthchais, g. of dùthchas.
dùthchas, nm. native place, nativity.

E.

each, nm. horse.
Eachann, pnm. Hector.
eagal, nm. fear.
eaglais, nf. church.
eaglaisean, pl. of eaglais.
ealanta, a. ready, fluent.
Ealasaid, pnf. Elizabeth.
Eanraig, pnm. Henry.
earball, nm. tail.
Earrach, nm. spring.
eich, g. sg. and nom. pl. of each.
eilean, nm. island.

éirich, v. arise.
éiridh, v. fut. of eirich.
Eirinn, nf. Ireland.
Eirionn, g. of Eirinn.
éisd, v. listen.
éisg, g. of iasg.
Eóghann, pnm. Hugh, Ewen.
Eòin (commonly Iain), pnm. John.
eòin, g. sg. and nom. pl. of eun.
eun, nm. bird.
euslan, a. unwell, infirm.

F.

fada, a. long.
fàg, v. leave.
faic, v. see, look.

faiceam, v. let me see.
faigh, v. get, find
fairge, nf. sea.

114 GAELIC GRAMMAR.

falamh, a. empty.
falbh, vn. going.
falt, nm. and nf. hair.
fan, v. stay, abide, remain.
fang, nf. sheepfold.
faing, d. of fang.
fann, a. weak, faint.
faobhar, nm. edge.
faoin, a. silly, gay.
fàs, v. grow.
fear, nm. man, any masc. individual, person or thing, one.
fearail, a. manly.
fearann, nm. land.
Fearchar, pnm. Farquhar.
fearg, nf. anger.
feargach, a. angry.
Fearghus, pnm. Fergus.
feasgar, nm. evening.
féidh, g. sg. and nom. pl. of fiadh.
feòir, g. of feur.
feòraich, v. ask.
feuch, v. see, try.
feum, nm. need.
feumail, a. needful.
feur (No. fiar), nm. grass.
feusag (No. fiasag), nf. beard.
fheara, voc. pl. of fear.
fhir, voc. of fear.

fhuair, v. got, found.
fiacaill, nf. tooth.
fiaclan, pl. of fiacaill.
fiadh, nm. deer.
fiodh, nm. wood.
fìon, nm. wine.
Fionghall, pnf. Flora.
fìor, a. and unatt. pref. true.
fios, nm. information.
fir, g. sg. and nom. pl. of fear.
fiùran, nm. blooming youth.
fiùrain, pl. of fiùran.
fleasgach, nm. young (unmarried) man.
fliuch, a. wet.
foghainteach, a. competent.
foghlum, nm. learning.
foghluimte, va. learned.
fosgail, v. open.
fraoch, nm. heather.
fras, nf. shower.
frasach, a. showery.
freagair, v. answer.
freagradh, nm. answer.
fuachd. nm. and nf. cold.
fuaim, nf. noise, sound.
fuar, a. cold.
fuaran, um. spring, fountain.
fuasgail, v. unloose.
fuilteach, a. bloody.

G.

gabh, v. take.
gabhadh, v. let — take.
gabhar, nf. goat.
gaduiche, nm. thief.
Gaidheal, pnm. Gael.
Gàidhlig, pnf. Gaelic.
gàir, v. laugh.
gàire, nm. and nf. laugh.
gairm, nf. call.
gairm, v. call.
gaisgeach, nm. hero.
gaoth, nf. wind.
gaoithe, g. of gaoth.
gaoith, d. of gaoth.
gaothar, a. windy.
gàradh, nm. garden.

garg, a. rough, fierce.
garga, pl. of garg.
gàd, nm. bar (of iron).
geal, a. white.
gealladh, nm. promise.
gearan, nm. complaint, complaining.
geàrr, v. cut.
gearradh, vn. cutting.
gearraidh, fut. of gèarr.
gearrar, v. will be cut.
geata, nm. gate.
geataichean, pl. of geata.
geug, nf. bough.
geugan, pl. of geug.
geum, v. low (as a cow).

geum, nm. bellow.
geur, a. sharp.
gheibh, v. will get.
ghlacadh, v. would catch and was caught.
gille, nm. lad.
gillean, pl. of gille.
Gill-easpuig, pnm. Archibald.
Giorsal, pnf. Grace (*Scotch*, Grizzel).
giùlain, v. carry.
giùlan, nm. carriage, bearing.
giullan, nm. boy.
giullain, g. sg. and nom. pl. of giullan.
glac, v. catch.
glac, nf. hollow, dell.
glaic, d. of glac.
glan, v. clean.
glais, d. of glas.
glas, a. grey.
Glascho, pnm. Glasgow.
glé, unatt. pref. very.
gleann, nm. glen, valley.
glic, a. wise.
glinn, pl. of gleann.

glinne, g. of gleann.
gliocas, nm. wisdom.
gnothuch, nm. business, matter.
gnùis, nf. countenance.
gobha, nm. smith.
gobhainn, g. of gobha.
goid, v. steal.
goirt, a. sore, bitter.
gòrach, a. foolish.
gorm, a. blue.
grad, a. quick.
grànda, a. ugly.
greusaich, nm. shoemaker.
grinn, a. elegant, neat.
Griogair, pnm. Gregor.
gruaidh, nf. cheek.
gruaidhean, pl. of gruaidh.
gruaim, nf. gloom.
gruagach, nf. maiden.
gual, nm. coal.
gualann, nf. shoulder.
guaillnean, pl. of gualann.
guil, v. weep.
gùn, nm. gown.
guth, nm. voice.

I.

Iain (Eòin), pnm. John.
iarunn, nm. iron.
iarr, v. seek, ask.
iasg, nm. fish.
iasgair, nm. fisher.
iasgairean, pl. of iasgair.
iath, v. hover around.
iathadh, vn. hovering around.
ìm, nm. butter.
ime, g. of ìm.
imich, v. go, depart.
inneau, nm. anvil.

innis, v. tell.
innsidh, fut. of innis.
innseadh, vn. telling.
iochd, nf. compassion, pity.
iochdmhor, a. pitiful, compassionate.
iolach, nf. shout.
iomair, v. row.
ionad, nm. place.
is, sv. is, are, etc.
Iseabal, pnf. Isabella.
ith, v. eat.

L.

là, nm. day.
labhair, v. speak.
labhairt, vn. speaking.
Lachann, pnm. Lachlan.
ladarna, a. impudent.
làidir, a. strong.

laimh, d. of làmh.
làir, nf. mare.
làithean, pl. of là.
làmh, nf. hand.
làmhan, pl. of làmh.
laoch, nm. hero.

laochan, nm. little hero.
laogh, nm. calf.
laoigh, pl. of laogh.
laoidh, nm. hymn, lay.
latha, g. of là.
leabaidh, nf. bed.
leabhair, g. of leabhar.
leabhar, nm. book.
leabhraichean, pl. of leabhar.
leac, nf. flagstone, school slate.
leag, v. knock down.
leagte, va. knocked down.
lean, v. follow.
leanabh, nm. child.
leisg, a. lazy.
leugh, v. read.
leughamaid, v. let us read.
leum, v. leap.
liath, a. grey, grey haired.
lic, d. of leac.
lion, v. fill.

lion, nm. net.
lion, nm. quantity, number.
lionadh, v. was filled.
lionmhor, a. plentiful.
litir, nf. letter.
litreach, g. of litir.
litrichean, pl. of litir.
loch, nm. loch.
Loch-Odha, pnm. Loch-Awe.
loisg, v. burn.
lom, a. bare.
lomairt, vn. clipping.
long, nf. ship.
luath, a. quick, swift.
luaidh, nm. and nf. darling.
luch, nf. mouse.
luchag, nf. little mouse.
luinge, g. of long.
luinneag, nf. ditty.
luinneig, d. of luinneag.
lunndaire, nm. lazy fellow.

M.

mac, nm. son.
machair, nf. plain.
madadh, nm. dog.
maduinn, nf. morning.
maide, nm. stick.
maighstir, nm. master.
maigheach, nf. hare.
mair, v. last, continue.
Màiri, pnf. Mary.
mall, a. slow.
Mànus, pnm. Magnus.
maol, a. bald, hornless.
marbh, v. kill.
marbh, a. dead.
marcaich, v. ride.
Marsali, puf. Marjory.
mart, nf. cow.
math (maith), a. good.
màthair, nf. mother.
màthar, g. of màthair.
meadhon, nm. middle.
meall, v. deceive.
meanglan, nm. branch.
meanglain, pl. of meanglan.
meas, nm. fruit.
mèilich, v. bleat.

meud (No. miad), nm. extent, size.
meur (No. miar), nm. and nf. finger.
mhic, voc. of mac.
mi-bheusach, a. unmannerly.
mic, g. of mac.
milis, a. sweet.
millte, va. spoiled.
min, a. smooth.
mine, gf. and pl. of min.
minidh, nm. shoemaker's awl.
ministir, nm. minister.
mionaid, nf. minute.
mionaidean, pl. of mionaid.
mir, nm. bit, piece.
mnathan, n. pl. of bean.
monadh, nm. mountain.
monaidh, g. of monadh.
mór, a. large, great, big.
móra, pl. of mór.
Mór, pnf. Sarah, Marion.
Mórag, pnf. little Sarah or Marion.
móran, nm. much, many.
mortair, nm. murderer.

VOCABULARY. 117

muc, nf. pig, sow.
muineal, nm. neck.
muir, nf. sea.

mulad, nm. sadness.
mullach, nm. top.
Murchadh, pnm. Murdoch.

N.

naigheachd, nf. news.
naimhdean, pl. of nàmhaid.
nàmhaid, nm. enemy, foe.
nathair, nf. serpent.
nead, nm. and nf. nest.
neapaicinn, nm. and nf. napkin.
neart, nm. strength.
neirt, g. of neart.

nì, nm. thing (NNii).
nì, v. will do (Nii).
Niall, pnm. Neil.
nigh, v. wash.
nighean, nf. daughter, maiden.
nighin, g. of nighean.
nitear, v. will be done.

O.

obair, nf. work.
òg, a. young.
òga, pl. of òg.
oidhche, nf. night.
òig, gm. of òg.
òige, gf. of òg.
òige, nf. youth.
òigear, nm. young man.
òigh, nf. maiden.
òighe, g. of òigh.
òl, v. drink.

òl, vn. drinking.
onoir, nf. honour, renown.
òr, nm. gold.
òraid, nf. speech.
òran, nm. song.
òrd, nm. hammer.
òrdugh, nm. command, order.
osnaich, nf. sighing.
othaisg, nf. hog (one-year-old sheep).

P.

Pàdruig, pnm. Patrick.
pàigh, v. pay.
pailte, a. plentiful.
paipear, nm. paper.
pàisde, nm. child.
Para, pnm. Patrick.
peann, nm. pen.
Peigi, pnf. Peggy, Margaret.
pige, nm. jar, pitcher.
pill, v. return, turn.
pilltinn, vn. returning.

piobaire, nm. piper.
piseag, nf. kitten.
piuthar, nf. sister.
pòiste, va. married.
poit, nf. pot.
Pòl (Pàl), pnm. Paul.
poll, nm. bog, mire.
pòs, v. marry.
preas, nm. bush.
pris, g. of preas.
priosan, nm. prison.

R.

rach, v. go.
rachainn, v. I would go.
rachamaid, v. let us go.
radan, nm. rat.
raimh, pl. of ràmh.
ràinig, v. reached.

ràmh, nm. oar.
Raonull, pnm. Ronald.
rathad, nm. road, way.
reamhar, a. fat.
reamhra, g. sg. f. and pl. of reamhar.

reic, v. sell.
riabhach, a. brindled.
rìbhinn, nf. pretty girl.
rinn, v. did.
riombal, nm. circle.
ro, unatt. pref. rather.
Rob, pnm. Robert.
robh, v. was, were.
ròs, nm. rose.
ròsan, pl. of ròs.
ròpa, nm. rope.
ròpan, pl. of ròpa.

ruadh, a. reddish-brown.
ruaidh, gm. of ruadh.
Ruaraidh, pnm. Rory, Roderick.
rud, nm. thing.
ruith, v. run.
ruith, vn. running.
rùisg, v. strip, bare.
rùisgte, va. bared.
rùn, nm. dear, beloved.
rùin, voc. of rùn.

S.

sabaid, nf. fight.
sabhull, nm. barn.
saighdear, nm. soldier.
saighdearan, pl. of saighdear.
salach, a. dirty.
salm, nf. psalm.
samhach, nf. haft, handle.
samhradh, nm. summer.
samhraidh, g. of samhradh.
saoithreach, a. industrious.
saor, nm. wright.
saoir, g. of saor.
Sasunn, pnm. England.
seall, v. look.
sean, a. old.
seanair, nm. grandfather.
seanmhair, nf. grandmother.
sèap (No. siap), v. sneak.
searbh, a. bitter.
searg, v. wither.
searmoin, nf. sermon.
searrach, nm. foal.
seas, v. stand.
seasmhach, a. steadfast.
sèid, v. blow.
seillean, nm. bee.
sèimh, a. mild, gentle.
seinn, v. sing.
seinn, vn. singing.
seirm, v. ring.
seòl, nm. sail.
seòl, v. sail.
seòladh, vn. sailing.
seòlta, a. cunning.
Seònaid, pnf. Janet.

Seumas, pnm. James.
sgaiteach, a. sharp, cutting.
sgaoil, v. spread.
sgaoilte, va. spread.
sgeir, nf. rock in the sea, skerry.
sgeul, nm. tale, story.
sgeulachd, nf. tale, story.
sgian, nf. knife.
sgine, g. of sgian.
sgiobair, nm. skipper.
sgiobalta, a. tidy, trig.
sgìth, a. weary, tired.
sglèat (No. sgliat), nm. and nf. slate.
sglèatair, nm. slater.
sglèatan, pl. of sglèat.
sgliat, see sglèat.
sgliatair, see sglèatair.
sgoil, nf. school.
sgoilear, nm. scholar.
sgoilearan, pl. of sgoilear.
sgòrnan, nm. thrapple.
sgread, nm. scream.
sgrìobh, v. write.
sgrìobhadh, vn. writing.
sguab, v. sweep.
sguabte, va. swept.
sguir, v. stop, cease.
sìd, nm. and nf. weather.
sil, v. drop, rain.
Sìlis, pnf. Cicely or Julia.
Sìne, pnf. Jane.
sinnsear, nm. ancestry.
sinnsir, g. of sinnsear.

VOCABULARY. 119

sloda, n. and a. silk.
siol, nm. seed.
sionnach, nm. fox.
siubhail, v. depart, die.
siùil, g. sg. and nom. pl. of seòl.
slàinte, nf. health.
slait, d. of slat.
slat, nf. rod, switch.
sluagh, nm. people.
smuoinich, v. think.
smaoin(t)eachadh, vn. thinking.
smeòrach, nf. mavis, thrush.
snaim, nm. knot.
snàmh, v. swim.
snàmh, vn. swimming.
sneachd, nm. snow.
socair, a. easy, comfortable.
soilleir, a. clear, bright.
soitheach, nm. vessel.
Somhairle, pnm. Somerled or Samuel.
soraidh, nf. compliments.
spàin, nf. spoon.

spéis, nf. fondness, regard.
spion, v. snatch, pluck, pull.
sporran, nm. purse.
srac, v. tear.
srath, nm. strath.
srathan, pl. of srath.
sròin, d. of sròn.
sròn, nf. nose.
sruith, g. of sruth.
sruth, nm. stream.
sruthan, nm. streamlet.
stàbull, nm. stable.
stad, v. stop, stay.
staidhir, nf. stair.
stoirm, nf. storm.
stiùir, v. steer.
stùc, nf. peak.
stùcan, pl. of stùc.
suas, up.
subhach, a. jolly.
suidh. v. sit.
sùil, nf. eye.
sùilean, pl. of sùil.
sùrd, nm. eager exertion.

T.

tabhannaich, nf. barking of dogs.
taighe, g. of tigh.
tàir, nf. reproach.
tàirneanach, nm. thunder.
taitneach, a. pleasing.
tana, a. thin, shallow.
taobh, nm. side.
taom, v. pour out.
tapaidh, a. clever.
tasdan, nm. shilling.
té, nf. feminine individual person or thing, one.
teadhair, nf. tether.
teagasg, vn. teaching.
teanga(dh), nf. tongue.
teann, a. firm, close, binding.
teich, v. flee.
téid, v. will go.
teine, nm. fire.
tha, sv. is, are, etc.
thàinig, v. came.
thairis, over.

thatar, v. it is being, they are.
théid, v. will go.
thig, v. will come.
thogadh, v. would lift.
thoir, v. give, take.
thubhairt, v. said.
thug, v. gave, took.
thugamaid, v. let us give.
thuirt, thubhairt syncopated.
tig, v. will come.
tigh, nm. house.
tighean, pl. of tigh.
tigh-òsda, nm. public-house.
tilg, v. throw.
till, v. return.
tinn, a. sick.
tionndaidh, v. turn about.
tionndamaid, v. let us turn.
tioram, a. dry.
tiormaich, v. dry.
tìr, nf. land.
tobar, nm. well, fountain.
tog, v. lift.

togamaid, v. let us lift.
togte, va. lifted.
toilichte, va. satisfied, pleased.
toir, v. will give.
tòir, nf. pursuit.
toiseach, nm. front, stem, beginning ; air toiseach, in front.
tòisich, v. begin.
tòisichear, v. will be begun.
toll, nm. hole.
toll, v. bore.
tom, nm. knoll.
toman, nm. little knoll.
Tómas, pnm. Thomas.
Tormaid, pnm. Norman.

treabh, v. plough.
treud, nm. flock, herd.
trod, v. scold.
trom, a. heavy.
trombaid, nf. trumpet.
trombaide, g. of trombaid.
truagh, a. wretched, miserable.
truaigh, voc. m. of truagh.
tuagh, nf. axe.
tuaigh, d. of tuagh.
tuathanach, nm. farmer.
tubh, v. thatch.
tubhadh, vn. thatching.
tuit, v. fall.
tunnag, nf. duck.

U.

uaine, a. green.
uair, nf. hour, time.
uairean, pl. of uair.
uamhasach, a. awful.
uan, nm. lamb.
uasal, a. noble, gentle.
Uilleam, pnm. William.
ùine, nf. time.

uinneag, nf. window.
uisge, nm. water.
ultach, nm. armful.
umhail, a. obedient.
ùr, a. new.
ùra, pl. of ùr.
urchair, nf. shot.
ùrlar, nm. floor.

VOCABULARY. 121

ENGLISH-GAELIC.

Note.—The letters in brackets indicate the classes which Nouns follow when they are declined.

A.

Alexander, Alasdair, pnm.
anvil, innean, nm.
armful, ultach, nm. (b).

ask, iarr, v.
awaken, dùisg, v.
axe, tuagh, nf. (a).

B.

back, druim, nm. (b).
bad, dona, a.
bag, poca, nm. (d).
bank, bruach, nf. (a).
bard, bàrd, nm. (a).
bean, pònair, nf. (d).
beard, feusag, nf. (b).
beautiful, bòidheach, a.
bee, seillean, nm. (b), ¶ 344.
bell, clag, nm. (a), ¶ 334.
ben, beinn, nf., g. beinne.
big, mór, a.
bird, eun, nm. (a), ¶ 337.
birds, eòin.
black, dubh, a.
blind man, dall, nm. (a), ¶ 335.
blood, fuil, nf., g. fola (b).
blow, buille, nm. and nf. (d).
blue, gorm, a.
boat, bàta, nm. (f).
bold, treun, a.

bonnet, boineid, nf. (d).
book, leabhar, nm., pl. leabhraichean.
bottle, botul, nm. (b).
bottom, grunnd, nm. (a).
boy, giullan, nm. (b).
branch, geug, nf. (a), ¶ 337;
 meanglan, nm. (b).
break, bris, v.
breeches, brigis, nf. (d).
bridge, drochaid, nf. (d).
bright, ùr, a.
bring, toir, tabhair, v.
brother, bràthair, nm. (g), ¶ 360.
brought, thug, v.
brown, donn, a.
build, tog, v.
bull, tarbh, nm. (a).
burn, loisg, v.
butter, ìm, nm. (a).
buy, ceannaich, v.

C.

calf, laogh, nm. (a).
came, thàinig, v.
carve, snaidh, v.
catch, glac, v.
chair, cathair, nf. (f).
chapter, caibideal, nm. (b), ¶344.
cheese, càise, nm. (a).
chest, ciste, nf. (h).
child, leanabh, nm., g. leinibh.
children, clann, nf., (a), ¶ 335.

church, eaglais, nf. (d).
clothes, aodach, nm. (b).
cloud, neul, nm. (a), ¶ 337.
coat, còta, nm. (f).
cold, fuar, a.
colour, dath, nm. (c).
company, buidheann, nf., ¶ 346.
country, dùthaich. nf. (e).
cow, bò, nf. (irregular).
cut, gèarr, v.

122 GAELIC GRAMMAR.

D.

dark, dorcha, a.
day, là, nm.; pl. làithean.
deceive, meall, v.
deep, domhain, a.
dell, glac, nf. (a).
desert, tréig, v.
desert, fàsach, nm. (b)., pl. -aichean.
dinner, dinneir, nf., g. -each, pl. -an.

dirty, salach, a.
dog, cù, nm. (irregular).
door, dorus, nm., pl. dorsan.
drink, deoch, nf.
drink, òl, v.
drop, boinne, nm. and nf. (h).
drown, bàth, v.
dry, tioram, a.

E.

ear, cluas, nf. (a).
empty, falamh, a.
eat, v. ith.

end, ceann, nm. (a), ¶ 339;
crioch, nf. (a), ¶ 340. at the end, aig ceann.

F.

faithful, dìleas, a.
fall, tuit, v.
farmer, tuathanach, nm. (b).
fat, reamhar, a., ¶ 369.
father, athair, nm. (g).
fear, eagal, nm.
feather, ite, nf. (d).
field, achadh, nm. (b), pl. -aidhean.
fight, cog, v., cath. n.
fill, llon, v.
finger, corrag, nf. (b), meur, nf. (a), ¶ 337.
fish, iasg, nm. (a), ¶ 338.
fishes, iasgan, n. pl.

fisherman, iasgair, nm. (d).
flail, suiste, nf. (d); buailtean, nm. (b), ¶ 344.
flat, còmhnard, réidh, a.
fling, tilg, v.
flood, tuil, nf. (a), ¶ 361.
floor, ùrlar, nm. (b).
flow, ruith, v.
food, biadh, nm.
foolish, gòrach, a.
foot, cas, nf. (a).
fresh, ùr, a.
friend, caraid, nm. (d); pl. càirdean.
frock, gùn, nm. (a), ¶ 361.

G.

Gael, Gaidheal, pnm. (b).
get, faigh; fhuair, did get.
girl, caileag, nf. (b).
give, tabhair, toir, thoir, v.
glen, gleann, nm.; pl. glinn and gleanntan.
glitter, soillsich, v.
go, rach, v. will go, théid.
got, fhuair, v.

good, math and maith, a.
grandfather, scanair, nm. (d).
grass, feur, nm. (a), ¶ 337.
great, mór, a.
green, uaine, a.
grey, glas, liath, a.
ground, làr, nm. (a).
grow, fàs, v.

H.

haddock, adag. nf. (b).
hair, falt, nm. and nf. (a), ¶ 334.

hand, làmh, nf. (a).
hammer, òrd, nm. (a), ¶ 334.

VOCABULARY. 123

hang, croch, v.
hard, cruaidh, a. (a).
hare, maigheach, nf. (b).
head, ceann, nm. (a), ¶ 339.
hear, cluinn, v.
heard, chuala, v.
hearing, cluinntinn, vn.
heart, cridhe, nm. (b).
heather, fraoch, nm. (a).
heavy, trom, a., ¶¶ 370, 334.
hen, cearc, nf. a. ¶ 339.

hero, laoch, nm. (a).
hide, ceil, v.
high, àrd, a.
hoist, tog, v.
hole, toll, nm. (a), ¶ 334.
honest, còir, ionraic, a.
horse, each, nm. (a), ¶ 343.
house, tigh, nm ; g. taighe.
hum, srann, nf. (a), ¶ 344.
hungry, acrach, a.

K.

key, iuchair, nf. (f).
knife, sgian, nf. ; g. sgìne.

knock down, leag, v.
knoll, cnoc, nm. (a), ¶ 334.

L.

lad, gille, nm. (d).
lame, crùbach, a.
land, tìr, nf. (a).
large, mór, a.
leaf, duilleag, nf. (b).
leave, fàg, v. -ail, vn.
leg, cas, nf. (a), ¶ 335.
letter, litir, nf. (f).
lid, clàr, nm. (a).

lift, tog, v.
light, solus, nm. (b).
likely, coltach, a.
listen, éisd, v.
little, beag, a.
load, luchd, nm. (c).
loch, loch, nm. (c).
long, fada, a.
look, amhairc, v.

M.

Magnus, Mànus, pnm.
maiden, maighdeann, nf. (b).
man, duine, nm. ; g. duine.
mare, làir, nf. (c) ; g. làrach.
Mary, Màiri, pnf.
mason, clachair, nm. (b).
matter, gnothuch, nm. (b), pl. -uichean.
mavis, smeòrach, nf. (b).
meat, biadh, nm.
meet, coinnich, v.

men, daoine, n. pl.
mend, càirich, v.
middle, meadhon, nm. (b).
milk, bainne, nm. (d).
mist, ceò, nm. ¶ 350.
mother, màthair, nf., ¶ 360.
mountain, monadh, nm. (b), pl. aidhean.
move, gluais, caraich, v.
moving, gluasad, vn.
music, ceòl, nm. (a), ¶ 336.

N.

nail, tarunn, nf., d. taruinn.
name, ainm, nm. (a).
needle, snàthad, nf. (b).
neighing, sitirich, nf. (c).
net, lìon, nm. ; pl. lìontan.

new, nuadh, ùr, a.
news, fios, nm. (c).
night, oidhche, nf. (d).
nose, sròn, nf., (a), ¶ 361.

124 GAELIC GRAMMAR.

O.

old, sean, a.
old man, seann-duine, nm.

open, fosgail.
oppress, sàraich, claoidh, v.

P.

people, muinntir, nm. (f).
pipe, pìob, nf. (e).
place, àite, nm. (d).
pleasant, taitneach, a.
poem, dàn, nm. (a).
point, bàrr, nm. (c).
portion, cuid, nf. (c).

pot, poit, nf. (a).
praise, mol, v.
prepare, deasaich, v.
price, prìs, nf. (a).
prow, toiseach, nm. (b).
put, cuir, v.

R.

read, leugh, v.
riches, beairteas, nm. (b).
river, amhainn, nf.; g. aimhne.

rod, slat, nf. (a).
row, iomair, v.
run, ruith, v.

S.

said, thubhairt, thuirt, v.
sail, seòl, nm. (a), ¶ 336.
sailor, maraiche, nm. (d).
savage, borb, a.
scales, lannan, n. pl.
school, sgoil, nf. (a).
sea, muir, nf. (b), ¶ 355.
seek, iarr, v.
sell, reic, v.
selling, reic, vn.
serpent, nathair, nf. (f).
sew, fuaighil, v.
sharp, geur, biorach, a.
sheep, caoraich, n. pl.
sheepfold, fang, nf. (a).
shepherd, buachaille, nm. (d).
shilling, tasdan, nm.
shine, dèarrs, v.
ship, long, nf. (a), ¶ 334.
shirt, léine, nf. (d), ¶ 361.
shoe, bròg, nf. (a).
shoelace, iall, nf. (a), ¶ 338.
shore, cladach, nm. (b).
sick, tinn, a.
side, taobh, nm. (a); pl. taobh-an.
sing, seiun, v.
singing, seinn. vn.

sit, suidh, v.
skin, feann, v.
sky, speur, nm. (c).
small, beag, a.
soldier, saighdear, nm. (b).
son, mac, nm.
song, òran, nm. (b).
sore, goirt, a.
sound, fuaim, nf. (a).
speak, bruidhinn, v.
speaking, bruidhinn, vn.
spend, cosd, v.
splendid, grinn, breagha, a.
spoil, mill, v.
spot, ball, nm. (a) ; pl. buill.
spread, sgaoil, v.
staff, bata, nm. (f).
steal, goid, v.
stick, maide, nm., pl. -an.
stone, clach, nf. (a), ¶ 335.
story, sgeul, nm. (a), ¶ 337 pl. -an.
strike, buail, v.
summer. samhradh, nm. (b).
sure, cinnteach, a.
sweet, milis, binn, a.
sword, claidheamh, nm. (b).

VOCABULARY. 125

T.

tail, earball, nm. (b).
tailor, tàilleur, nm. (b), ¶ 344.
take, gabh, v.
tale, sgeul, nm. (see story).
taste, blas, nm. (a).
taste, blais, v.
tell, innis, v.
thatch, tubh, v.
thick, tiugh, a.

thin, tana, a.
time, àm, nm. (d).
top, mullach, nm. (b).
torn, sracte, va.
town, baile, nm. (d), ¶ 361.
tree, craobh, nf. (a).
true, fìor, a.
trumpet, trombaid, nf. (d).
turn, tionndaidh, v.

V.

very, glé, unatt. pref.

voice, guth, nm.

W.

wall, balla, nm. (f), pl. -achan.
warm, blàth, a.
water, uisge, nm. (h).
wave, tonn, nm. (a), ¶ 334.
way, rathad, nm. (b).
weep, guil, v.
well, tobar, nm. (b), ¶ 345.
went away, dh'fhalbh, v.
wet, fliuch, a.
whelp, cuilean, nm. (b), ¶ 344.
white, geal, bàn, a.
whiting, fionnag, nf. (d), iasg-geal.

will go, théid, v.
wind, gaoth, nf. (a).
window, uinneag, nf. (d).
winter, geamhradh, nm. (b).
woman, bean, nf. ; g. mnatha.
wood, coille, nf. (d), ¶ 361.
word, facal, nm. (b),
work, obair, nf. ; g. oibre,
¶ 358.
wright, saor, nm. (a).
write, sgrìobh, v.

Y.

year, bliadhna, nf. (f).
yield, géill, v.

young, òg, a.
youth, òige, nf. (d).

SUGGESTIVE SCHEME OF LESSONS.

Note.—Teachers are enjoined to make frequent use of the blackboard and neglect no opportunity of giving vocal illustration. In doing the latter they should avoid provincialisms in pronunciation, when these are at variance with the spelling, *e.g. diag* when the spelling is *deug*. At the same time, it is open to them to point out differences between local pronunciation and that represented by the spelling. They should strictly avoid the use of the words "qualify" and "modify" in stating the relation of one word to another—as, when it is said, "The adjective qualifies the noun." The word following always *limits* the word preceding. Any other way of stating the case gives rise to confusion of ideas. Pupils should be made to write to dictation each exercise before passing on to the next lesson. In the following scheme the numerical figures refer to the paragraphs.

1-7. General discourse. Examples. Explanation of terms. 8-20. Discourse on spelling. Illustrations of disagreement between Pronunciation and Spelling in the English and other languages. Alphabetic devices in other languages. 21-30. The use of a Phonetic Alphabet. 31-32 (pass by 33-42), 43-45 (pass by 46-48). Illustrate 32 by written examples. 49-54. 55-61. 62-71. 72-84. REVISAL. Ex. Written examples with pronunciation being given, name the Low and High Consonants; the Long, Short, and Silent Vowels; the Diphthongs; Silent Consonants and Compound Consonants. Ex. Write to teacher's dictation, simple words illustrating the preceding classes of Vowels and Consonants. 85-98. Written and Vocal illustration of 93, 94, and 98. 99-101. Further examples. 102-106. Ditto. 107-121.

SUGGESTIVE SCHEME OF LESSONS. 127

Ditto. 122-129. Ditto. REVISAL. Ex. In sentences gleaned from the exercises, name the different mechanical changes, as, Synthesis, Aspiration, Euphony and Elision. 130-144. Further examples. 145-155. Devote particular care to 150. 156-163. Devote particular care to 158. Further examples. 164-167. Ex. Distinguish the Limiting words and those which they limit in 167. 168-172. 173-180. Devote particular care to 173 as much depends on the pupil's grasp of this ¶. REVISAL. Ex. Distinguish the Subjects, Predicates, Objects and the Parts of Speech and their Classes, Cases, etc., in past Exs. 181-192. Devote care to 183. 193-198. Ex. Appropriate Nouns in all their cases being given, place the correct Article before each. Ex. Introduce Prepositions before the same Nouns. 199-201. 202-207. 208-220. 221-228. Ex. Translate into Gaelic, Simple Sentences such as, "I will strike," "We struck," "You stood," etc., using Verbs out of past Exs., and all the Pronouns. 229-235. Ex. Translate into Gaelic, Phrases such as, "This horse," "Yon dog," etc., using Nouns out of past Exs. 236-239. Ex. Translate into Gaelic, Phrases such as, "My horse," "Their cow," etc., using Nouns out of past Exs. 240-245. Ex. Translate into Gaelic, Phrases such as, "To me," "From her," etc., using all the Pronouns and Prepositions. Ex. Analyse the Prepositional Pronouns into their separate elements. 246-247. Exs. As last. REVISAL. Ex. Distinguish the Parts of Speech and their Classes, etc., in past Exs. 248-251. Ex. Translate into Gaelic, Words and Phrases such as, "Me," "You," etc., with the correct Unaccented Emphasising Suffix; "Myself," "My own dog," "Her own fat hen," etc., using Nouns and Adjectives out of past Exs. 252-255 and Table of Cardinal Numerals. Ex. Translate into Gaelic, Phrases such as, "33 ducks," teacher giving correct Plural forms of the Nouns used. Ex. Make complete Table of Cardinal Numerals up to 200, with and without a Noun. Translate into Gaelic, several Numerals ranging from 200 to 1000, with and without a Noun. 256-259 and Table of Ordinal Numerals. Treat similarly to last. 260-262. Ex. Translate into Gaelic, Sentences such as, "I will be hung," "James was lifted," etc., using Verbs in 262. 263-274. Carefully impress pupils with the fact that the Verb *limits* the Particles which precede it. Ex. Translate into Gaelic, Sentences such as, "Did he strike," "Will I take," etc., using Verbs in 274. 275-281. Ex. Translate into Gaelic, Sentences such as "Will you be good," "Were they bad," etc., using Adjectives out of past Exs., and all the Pronouns. 282-286. Ex. Translate into Gaelic, Sentences such as, "He is running," "We were reading," "The man was sleeping," etc., using Verbs in 286. 287-294. REVISAL. Ex. Distinguish the Parts of Speech, their Classes, etc., in the past Exs. 295-307. 308-313. 314-316. 317-318. Ex. Write Paradigms of certain Regular Verbs, using the Numerical Figures to represent Tense, Voice, Mood, and Mode. Ex. Write certain Regular Verbs in all their Phases, preceded by the Particles, and give translation. 319-326. 327-332. 333-340. 341-346. 347-351. 352-356. 357-362. 363. Ex. Write Paradigms of certain Nouns, their Classes being stated, with Prepositions and Article. 364-371. Ex. Write Paradigms of Nouns, their Classes being stated, with Prepositions, Articles, and Adjectives. 372. REVISAL. GENERAL REVISAL. 32-48. Intelligent Gaelic-speaking pupils should be encouraged to practise Phonetic Writing, and even to take down Colloquialisms Phonetically; e.g. KAA VʜL U DOLL for C' àite 'bheil thu 'dol.

INDEX TO CONTENTS.

PREFACE,	3
INTRODUCTION,	5
SECTION I. WORDS IN ISOLATION,	7
SECTION II. WORDS IN COMPOSITION,	22
SECTION III. WORD FORMATION AND DEVELOPMENT,	31
SECTION IV. THE FUNCTIONS OF WORDS,	34
SECTION V. THE INFLECTIONS OF WORDS,	83
TABLE OF NUMERALS,	106
VOCABULARY—GAELIC-ENGLISH,	109
ENGLISH-GAELIC,	121
SUGGESTIVE SCHEME OF LESSONS,	126

PRINTED BY ARCHIBALD SINCLAIR, CELTIC PRESS, GLASGOW

www.ingramcontent.com/pod-product-compliance
Lightning Source LLC
Chambersburg PA
CBHW020109170426
43199CB00009B/457